Isabelle Hamley is Theological Adviser to the House of Bishops and was formerly Chaplain to the Archbishop of Canterbury. She has long been concerned with questions of justice, mercy and restoration, having been a probation officer before ordination and ministering subsequently amid the diversity of parish life. Her books include *The Bible and Mental Health* (2020), which she edited with Christopher C. H. Cook, and *Unspeakable Things Spoken* (2019). *Embracing Justice* is her first Lent book.

EMBRACING JUSTICE

Isabelle Hamley

First published in Great Britain in 2021

Society for Promoting Christian Knowledge
36 Causton Street
London SW1P 4ST
www.spck.org.uk

British Library Cataloguing-in-Publication Data
A catalogue record for this book is available from the British Library

ISBN 978-0-281-08654-2
eBook ISBN 978-0-281-08655-9

Typeset by Fakenham Prepress Solutions, Fakenham, Norfolk NR21 8NL
First printed in Great Britain by Ashford Colour Press

Printed and bound in Great Britain by Clays Ltd, Elcograf S.p.A.

eBook by Fakenham Prepress Solutions, Fakenham, Norfolk NR21 8NL

Produced on paper from sustainable forests

To my grandfather, Jean,
who taught me to love justice

'Justice and only justice you shall pursue.' (Deuteronomy 16.20)

'That's not fair!' (Universal human cry from cradle to grave)

Contents

Contents

Foreword

The joy of the Christian faith is the hope – the promise – of a world transformed. The six weeks of Lent is a journey we travel together towards that world. From Ash Wednesday through to Maundy Thursday, the season of Lent guides us from human frailty into the glorious light of God's triumph over death.

Lent is also a time of reflection. It's traditionally a time when people give something up, a season of fasting. This Lent, I will be turning to Isaiah 58.6, which reads, 'Is not this the fast that I choose: to loose the bonds of injustice, to let the oppressed go free, and to break every yoke?'

The past few years have been ones where the calls for justice have been deafening. From the Me Too and Black Lives Matter movements, the earth is shaking with the cries of those seeking justice in an unjust world. The disproportionate impact of the Covid-19 pandemic on those who were already from marginalized communities – women, those who are disabled, people from UK Minority Ethnic communities – exposed much of the injustice that has made its home in the cracks of our society. The Archbishops' Commission on Housing, Church and Community noted the correlation between poor Covid outcomes and inadequate housing. The Reimagining Social Care Commission was launched shortly after care homes were decimated by the pandemic. It is clear we are living in a time of grave injustice, one which fails to see the image of God in each person, one where awful things happen – sometimes behind closed doors in dark, forgotten corners of the world, sometimes in plain sight for us all to see.

As we contemplate the ways in which our world falls so short of God's vision for us, it seems to me that Lent might also be a time for transformation, of moving from this old world into the new. As we retreat, we give ourselves time and space to be re-formed, like a caterpillar's metamorphosis – a time when we might step out of our old clothes of injustice and re-robe ourselves in the shining garb of the new kingdom. During Lent, we have the chance to walk towards the God who journeys towards us. Over forty days, we can move from our flawed humanness to our humaneness, from brokenness to wholeness, repentance into restoration.

I think we all know the outrage of unfairness, the indignation and fury that stirs in the gut when we feel wronged. A colleague of mine's father received a parking ticket in his early 20s. Convinced it was unjust, he fought it in court. Although he lost, this taste of fighting for justice, the outrage at injustice, led him to do a law conversion course, then find his vocation in a city law firm from which, after many years, he recently retired. We don't all have to become lawyers and judges, but each in our own way we are drawn towards the call: 'justice, justice you shall pursue' (cf. Deuteronomy 16.20).

When we are nurses or doctors caring for everyone on the ward regardless of wealth or status, we pursue justice. When we are mothers or fathers, teaching children about fairness and kind-ness, we are building a more just future. Whether we are teachers, cleaners, chefs, office workers – whatever we do, there is a way to do it with the pursuit of justice at its core when we look to God for guidance. There is always a way to transform our 'parking tickets' into a better world; there is always a way to embrace justice.

Justice might start with the individual heart, but it seeps through to the communities, systems and institutions we live in and uphold. It reaches into every facet of our interlinked society – from educa-tion to incarceration, housing to healthcare, culture to climate. As Christians, we are called to build communities that serve every person, regardless of who they are.

Justice is a godly thing. It is the opposite of the dehumanizing cruelty, the parody of justice, that Jesus faced on the cross. It is not vengeful, nor is it brutal. It goes hand in hand with mercy. As God meets our fallenness with his forgiveness, entering into the woundedness of his people; pierced by the jagged edges of our greed and anger; hung on the cross borne of our hatred and rejection – he is already making his justice afresh. The promise of the resurrection is that all things can be made new; nothing is beyond God's healing.

As, in the shadows of Lent, we dare to dream of the glorious light of the day of the resurrection, the day God pours himself out to make right what is wrong, make whole what is broken and perfect what is flawed, may we start to think about how we are invited to step into that world and God's work in the here and now. My challenge this Lent comes from Isaiah 56.1 – 'maintain justice, and do what is right, for soon my salvation will come, and my deliverance be revealed.'

+ + *Justin Cantuar*
Lambeth Palace, London

Acknowledgements

I would like to thank my colleagues and friends Anderson Jeremiah and Selina Stone, who helped me shape this book, and whose advice, knowledge and wisdom have contributed immensely to its writing.

Approaching justice

I grew up in a big family, with a brother and sister, but also a large, extended, always-present family of 50 first cousins just on my father's side (yes, you read this correctly, 50!). Most years we met as a big tribe for a few days, and those times were both the best and the worst of the year. Best, because they were full of laughter and games, of climbing trees and making dens, of midnight feasts and whispered scary stories in the dark. But they were also the worst, because we were constantly negotiating our place in the bigger tribe – age and gender made a difference, but far more than that, there were subtle differences in class and education that loomed larger as we grew older, and deepened the fault lines we could see between our parents. We were all one big family, but life had helped some and left others behind, and you could tell by our clothes, our words and our interests. It didn't take long for entire groups to gang up on others, and for some of the kids to be picked out as those who didn't fit in. Because I was one of the oldest, but also one with more financial means, more access to extracurricular activities, and I was more bookish and reserved, I was considered fair game. It wasn't fair. I resented being picked out, not fitting in with the easy camaraderie I imagined the others had without me. But of course, they also had their own cry. It wasn't fair that some of us had music lessons, regular holidays, even a passport, when the others didn't. It wasn't fair that a handful of us went to university, and others didn't. Fairness isn't a mathematical concept.

What *is* fair? What *is* just? A hankering for justice and fairness lurks everywhere in life, from a toddler not getting their way to the complex dynamics of international relationships, and in almost every page of Scripture. The answer, however, is elusive. Human beings are much better at recognizing what is not fair, what is unjust, than at agreeing on what would be, and making it happen. In the wake of the Covid-19 pandemic, questions of justice abound. Why do some die while others live? Why are there such differences in access to care, vaccines, oxygen even? Is it just to impose lockdowns and restrict liberty? Who should be required to physically go to work? Who shouldn't? Should the risks be reflected in pay? Covid-19, with the typical neutrality of a virus, knows no status, wealth or privilege, and attacks everyone. Yet the human ability to withstand this attack differs hugely depending on geography, social positioning, culture and political context. Covid-19 has magnified existing inequalities, and those have morphed into deep injustices. We face the same type of questions and disagreements when we speak of climate change, of economic systems, of territorial conflicts, of refugees and migration, or how to respond to crime.

Bringing injustice to light, recognizing and naming it matters; yet how to respond is more difficult, because of the huge complexity of local and global systems of relationships, politics and economics, which makes it almost impossible to address one aspect of injustice without a cascade of unintended consequences. Even if this complexity could be modelled and understood, and there was both will and power to respond, it would not necessarily help solve either global or local inequalities, because different cultures, political values and social systems shape very different visions of what is just, good or fair. 'Justice' may be a common goal, but how 'we', as human beings, define justice is not something we hold in common. Just as for me and my cousins, what is fair depends on where and how we live. Different visions of the common good, and what is acceptable in pursuing it, often collide and clash, and reduce the dreams of each group to whatever compromise they can all agree.

As Christians, we are no different. Our imagination of the common good, justice, rights and duties is shaped partly by our Scriptures and tradition. It is also shaped, however, by the cultures and philosophies that shape our lives, our politics and our belonging in time and place. We cannot stand outside of all these influences; what we can do however is examine them: lay our lives and stories alongside the story of God and his people in Scripture, and seek to listen to the questions that Scripture asks of our lives, and that our lives ask of Scripture. We can listen to Christians from other times and places who may understand the Scriptures in different ways, and ask what they might teach us.

The Bible is steeped in the language of justice, and the people of God, throughout Old and New Testaments, are called to do justice as a central aspect of their vocation. What justice is this, and how can it help us wrestle with doing justice for today? The Bible has no pat, one-size-fits-all answers. Like us, the writers and people of the story were immersed in cultures and systems that shaped their imagination and their vision. They wrestled with themselves, with one another and with God in trying to do justice. We can do the same today and wrestle with God and our conscience: we can enter the world of Scripture, walk alongside its people, and seek to listen to God speaking to us about what it means to be human and to live well together.

The Bible does not have one story of justice, it has many. It speaks of justice in many voices, which interweave and nuance one another. If we use only one story as a definitive statement on justice, we distort the biblical witness as a whole, and reduce justice to a monolithic concept, rather than a vocation to be worked out in every new time and place. And so we will look at several of these threads: justice in the creation accounts, justice as liberation, justice as building healthy communities, justice as relationship, justice as the reconfiguration of power. All of these together give a rich, textured picture of how God works with humanity to bring justice, wholeness and salvation to individuals and communities.

Beyond Scripture, we will listen to Christians from different parts of the world, and how they wrestle with justice in their contexts. Their words are reproduced faithfully; they may be challenging, uncomfortable, and sometimes even alien. Yet they are words from other parts of the Church, and they remind us that to seek justice is not an individual, private pursuit, but something we do together. We discern justice as a Church, and the different, sometimes conflicting voices all need to be heard and attended to so that our hearts are enlarged and we ask questions we would not think of alone.

Whether with Scripture or with today's world, everything starts with stories, rather than concepts, ideas or definitions. Scripture begins with stories, and everything it says refers to and reflects the wider arc of God's work of creation, salvation and redemption. This is particularly important when talking about justice, because stories are about people; they do not allow us to conceptualize or abstract what we are talking about, but keep the reality of the suffering caused by injustice at the forefront of our minds. They force us to keep looking into the eyes of those who suffer. Stories, however, are not tidy, and often leave us with more questions than answers. This is the genius of stories: with their ambiguities and unanswered questions, they invite us to continue to wrestle with the text, our consciences and the vocation of being a Christian for today. And this wrestling seems like a perfect task for Lent: an invitation to examine our lives truthfully, see the world more deeply, but, more than that, it is an invitation to prayer – for the Church, for the world, for those who are far and those who are near, that 'justice may roll down like waters, and righteousness like an ever-flowing stream' (Amos 5.24).

1

Paradise lost

In search of original justice

Justice in creation: Genesis 1—2

The image of God

It is easy to think of justice as remedying wrong, holding sinners to account, reaching for an ideal we can barely imagine. While this is entirely appropriate, it somehow reduces justice to a remedy for sin, something that has come out of the darkest and most negative parts of ourselves. Yet we cannot label something a wrong, injustice or inequality unless we have some vision of what life should be. The question then is, who decides what the 'right' picture is, and how? In Christian terms, this 'right' picture is not just remedial; it is not simply a picture of what life can and will be, some day. This picture is anchored much deeper, in the very fabric of creation, because it reflects the unchanging, deep nature of God. It is therefore logical to start thinking about justice by looking at the accounts of creation, and how they reveal the nature of God as a God of justice.

The stories[1] of Genesis 1 and 2 may seem far away, and quaint when put alongside the narratives of origins that we tell through science and biology. They relate a different kind of story, about who we are, who we are meant to be, and who God is. Human beings all tell stories about where they come from and how they fit into the order of the world. We have explanations for why the

---

1 I use the word 'story' to reflect the fact that these are told narratively, rather than using the categories of science or philosophy, and not to make any comment on truth or historicity.

world is the way it is, in its beauty and its pain. These explanations help us understand we are part of something bigger than ourselves; they give us a vision for life, and patterns for how to live it. They bring meaning to our lives. Yet these stories often have a darker side, too. Though we may not always be aware of it, the ways in which we make sense of life influence the ways in which we make sense of the life of someone else, someone with different experiences. Stories and narrative of meaning are powerful: they shape the world and social order, and they have the potential to be abused. The tendency is evident throughout history, as pseudo-science has been used to oppress and mistreat entire groups of people, whether through race-based slavery, claims of women's inferiority, or Nazism's Aryan race philosophy. Religion has been used to claim that wealth and prosperity are a sign of God's blessing on those who deserve it, thereby justifying the suffering of those who live in disadvantage and poverty. The ways we think today are not immune to the dangers, either: evolution and survival of the fittest can be used to justify social arrangements and differences of outcome between people, as can political theories around meritocracy, which argue that the rich deserve their wealth. Meanwhile, the ways in which we tell the history we claim as ours often shapes the claims we make on the present. The world of the Bible may be far removed from ours, yet in essence human beings have not changed much.

In the Ancient Near East, many stories about creation and the beginning of the world circulated, and they usually undergirded the claim of one special individual: the king, and his descendants. Kings were often said to be made in the image of God – the *only* human beings made in the image of God. 'Normal' people belonged to a different class, or sometimes different, hierarchized classes. In contrast, in Genesis, *all* human beings, plural, are made in the image of God. All of them! Not just the king, nor even people of status, and not just the men, but all, including (perhaps most shocking of all in a patriarchal culture) women. The challenge ran very deep.

So God created humankind in his image,
in the image of God he created them;
male and female he created them.
(Genesis 1.27)

There is no value difference between human beings. Whoever they are, they are made in the image of God, uniquely precious, with infinite dignity and worth. The Bible's challenge to surrounding philosophies was not to bring the kings down, but to bring everybody 'up'; not to devalue human beings, but to affirm their beauty and likeness to God. No human being has a greater claim than another: their equality is absolute. To use 'male and female' was a way to embrace the whole of humanity, a literary formula to stress both the completeness of what it says and the unity of humanity across its differences. In a world marked by sharp hierarchical distinctions, a world of slaves and masters, of victors and conquered, a world defined by patriarchy, this was revolutionary. In fact, it does not matter hugely when exactly Genesis 1 was written. In almost any context, this proclamation is challenging and subversive. The depth of challenge can be seen through the way many cultures have tried to redefine it, ignore it or propose reinterpretations that diminish its strength: despite the proclamation of radical equality, women have been considered inferior in most cultures that claimed Christianity as their roots for centuries; people of colour have often been treated in ways that deny their essential equality, dignity and worth even when reading Scripture side by side with those who oppress them.

Human beings have an infinite capacity for self-deception and selective hearing when it comes to the words of Scripture. Genesis proclaims that all humanity is made in God's image. Full stop. The fact that this is embedded in the story of creation, when the world was declared 'good', and its inhabitants 'very good', suggests that equality and justice are not an aspiration, but a baseline: treating every other human being as made in the image of God and fundamentally worthy of respect, dignity and equality is the very minimum, the starting point, in human relationships. This baseline is then threaded through any other talk of justice in Scripture:

we cannot speak of justice unless it is anchored in the nature of God as revealed in creation; and we cannot speak of justice unless we engage seriously with the fact that every single human being, however objectionable, unpleasant, strange, offensive, uncomfortable or different, is made in the image of God. Every human being, regardless of age, physical characteristics, abilities, choices, personalities, beliefs, contribution, deserts and so on, is made in the image of God.

The pattern of the image of God has profound implications. It affirms that justice can never be solely about economics or meeting basic needs; it is about dignity, worth and social goods like freedom, recognition, participation in society, decision-making, bodily and intellectual integrity. The rest of Scripture reflects this sense of the infinite worth of the human person, and how this needs to shape relationships. In the story of Noah, the image of God forms the basis of a prohibition on murder, and of God's 'reckoning for human life' (Genesis 9.5–6); the link here further suggests that to harm the image of God in a human being is therefore to harm God, too. It fails to respect the design of creation and the worth of each person. The letters of James (3.9–10) and 1 John (4.20) both refer to the image of God as a primary reason for honouring other human beings and speaking well of them. The story of creation sets up expectations and claims on human beings and their relationships and social arrangements. How this is transferred into practice is, of course, something that human beings have expressed in different ways and disagreed on profoundly.

The beauty of difference

Equality and dignity relate to justice, but equality and justice are not the same. Many disagreements over how to shape a 'just' society centre on how equality and difference are articulated. This relationship is clearly signalled in Genesis: diversity and difference (male and female) are an inherent part of being made in the image of God, yet held together in complete harmony. It is easy to get distracted by 'male and female' and what it means exactly; yet the primary point of the verse is not about sex or gender, but about unity in difference. Difference is acknowledged, while essential commonality – the image of God – establishes that difference does not affect value.

Human societies often struggle to hold difference in non-hierarchical ways. Difference does not have to be compared or ranked, yet human beings almost always respond by making comparisons. We might say to our children that different career choices are all OK, however academic or lucrative; but in practice, society values and rewards some far more than others. Hence there is some suspicion of slogans like 'equal but different', as they have been used, for instance, in segregationist contexts in South Africa and in the United States, to legitimize inequality of treatment. This is where things get complicated: instinctively, we know that to be fair means both to treat people equally and to be attentive to differential needs. How do you balance these two things? How do you attend to difference and otherness without turning difference into a judgement of value or worth? It is easy to have an implicit model or ideal of a human being, and rank real persons according to how well they conform to this ideal type.

The Genesis story challenges and reverses this tendency, by holding together dignity and difference. Difference is acknowledged, yet held within the image of God, so that difference is no bar to equality and worth, but a cherished aspect of humanity. Attending to difference may mean treating different people differently, but the source and the aim of how we relate should always be to honour the image of God found in the other. So, for instance, legal provisions are made that recognize the vulnerability of children: they are made in the image of God and just as valuable as adults, but their specific characteristics and stages of development mean that they need additional protection so that the image of God within them can be respected and protected. The tax system in most Western countries also acknowledges that diversity means that justice demands differential treatment: sliding scales of taxation are used to reflect the fact that those on low income pay tax out of what is their necessary income, things they need to survive, while those on higher incomes pay a higher amount of tax, which comes largely out of their disposable income. A straight percentage would not be fair or just, because its impact would be dramatically different on different groups. Genesis 1 sets up this dynamic tension between equality and difference right from the start of the story of God and his people. Furthermore, the accent put on diversity underscores the interdependence of humanity: it is *together* that they are made in the image of God.

A world of connections

Interdependence is rooted in Genesis 1, and reinforced in the parallel account of Genesis 2, the story of the creation of human beings in the garden. Just as in Genesis 1, human beings are both equal and interdependent: the words for 'man' and 'woman' appear at the same time in the story, once there are two of them. Before that, the human being is 'the adam', that is, the earth creature, the thing formed from the ground. God had taken earth, *adamah* in Hebrew, to make a human, *ha-adam*. The writer is playing with words, anchoring human beings to the earth they have been taken out of. Yet a single human, with no difference and no other to interact with, is lonely, a loneliness that not even divine presence can remedy. Difference is necessary for the earth creature to flourish. Another human is created from a rib – not the head, not the feet, but the middle of the body – and called a 'helper'. The word has often been abused to assume inferiority. Yet it is a word often used of God himself helping Israel, and denotes partnership. The earth creature has been given an equal, who is the same, yet profoundly different. They are 'man' and 'woman' in their difference, and yet in Hebrew, 'the adam' is used for the whole of humanity, rather than to stress gender or sex. The whole of humanity is tethered to the ground, anchored in the natural world.

The interdependence of people and nature is everywhere in Genesis 1–2. Human beings do not appear until verse 26 in Genesis 1: they are not the centre of everything, and the story says much more about the world as a whole than about humans. Genesis 2 focuses more narrowly on humanity, but nature is everywhere. It is worth pausing here, and asking, how do we extend questions of justice beyond inter-human relationships, to form an interwoven pattern with the whole of creation? If human beings are made in the image of God, what does this say of the value and worth of the place within which God has set them? What does the fact that these precious bearers of the divine image cannot live without the resources of, and appropriate relationship to, the natural world say about the worth of this world?

In Genesis 1, God declares every part of creation, 'good', and the whole of creation together, 'everything that he had made' (1.31), 'very good'. The evaluation 'very good' comes after a statement on the interdependence of creation in verses 28–30, the way in which it forms a habitat that can sustain the life of animals and humans. What kind of claims and responsibilities does God's verdict of goodness on creation place on human beings? Western countries have long treated nature as if it was made primarily for them to use. Genesis 1 is not quite so straightforward. First, this is poor logic: if we are going to claim that being made in the image of God means that human beings are special and must be respected, then surely the natural world being declared 'very good' by God also creates an obligation to respect it. Second, animals are also 'given' the earth for their benefit, so that human beings are not unique, but part of a much wider system.

Genesis 2 further illustrates this. God creates the earth first, yet there was 'no one to till it' (2.5) – just like the earth creature will have no one to help him in 2.20. Human beings are given responsibilities to tend to creation and care for it early on (2.15). While human beings are presented as unique and different from other creatures, their difference is nuanced by interdependence and confers responsibilities. The human tendency to see ourselves as having 'rights' over creation, rather than responsibilities towards it, is a distortion of the picture in Genesis, and of the later story. Throughout the Old Testament, human beings' responsibility to, and impact on, the land is highlighted again and again. The law books of Exodus, Leviticus and Deuteronomy give proactive instructions on how to care for the land, and warnings that human actions affect the land itself.

Discovering God in creation

A picture is emerging of humanity, gifted with the dignity of free will, a dignity that brings together freedom and responsibility. They are not children, cared for by a doting relative, but people made in the image of God, endowed with the ability and responsibility to live well and shoulder burdens of care towards creation and one another. The nature of God gradually emerges through the story. First, the picture is one of overwhelming generosity and abundance. Creation is not composed of the bare minimum, but brims over with beauty and diversity. There are more colours, more plants, more animals, more ecosystems than strictly 'needed'. Creation is not utilitarian, and neither people nor animals are reduced to survival and basic needs. God's actions are marked by generosity: not just in physical provision, but in risk-taking and sharing his own image and responsibilities. Human beings are not controlled or subjugated, nor are they created for the use and benefit of God (unlike in many ancient stories where human beings are often created as slaves for the gods); their creation and that of the earth is a free gift, a sharing of life and goodness by the Creator. Justice is inherent in the blueprint of creation, through equality, care and dignity, and the subtext of creation underlies appeals to God for justice throughout Scripture, particularly in the psalms.

If human beings embody the image of God on earth, then the invitation is for them to display the same kind of abundant generosity, trust and life-giving relationships. Just like God, human beings are not meant to be utilitarian. This may be most obvious in the inclusion of the Sabbath within the creation narrative (2.1–3). After all his work, God rests, and this resting will be taken into rules for abundant life for human beings. Resting is hallowed and blessed: life is not ruled by work, productivity and efficiency. Work gives dignity and reflects a God who works, six days out of seven. Creativity in human beings reflects God's image; yet work and production do not define the whole of God. Work stops, and the stopping is hallowed as nothing else was, which prompts questions about the worth of human persons, and care for creation, which rests in equal measure.

Questions for reflection

1 What stories/explanations do you have for how the world is
 organized? For inequality in society, locally and worldwide?
2 How do/could you consciously honour the 'image of God' in
 the people you meet? In the people whose stories you see on
 the news? Are there people you struggle to see the 'image of
 God' in? What might help?
3 What parts of your life are obviously interdependent with the
 wider creation? How might you become more conscious of
 your impact on nature, and its impact on you?

When good goes bad: Genesis 3

Key text: Genesis 3.1–21

A breakdown in relationships

With such a wonderful picture as Genesis 1—2, the natural question is, 'Then how could things go so wrong?' How did this picture of justice and abundance get corrupted into gaping inequality, poverty, abuse, injustice and oppression? Genesis 3 answers these questions theologically. Genesis 2 had zoomed in, from the universal picture of chapter 1, on to one specific human couple, a couple who represent every human being in their choices, feelings and actions. It is a well-known story: a man and a woman (not called by name yet) live in the garden of delight, in harmony with nature, with God and with each another. They are comfortable with who they are, happy to be seen and known by God and each another. There is no inequality or hierarchy between them, they both speak, act and make decisions. There is only one restriction on their lives: they are told not to eat 'of the tree of the knowledge of good and evil' (2.16–17). There is nothing here to suggest that these two humans did not know right from wrong, or good from evil; it is simply that the tree was forbidden. Human beings did not have full control of everything. God placed limits on them, not gratuitously, but out of loving care. It is God who defines good and evil, and teaches his people – much like loving parents help guide children so that they learn at the right pace, with kindness and forgiveness for mistakes, but also so that right and wrong are set within relationships: they are not primarily 'concepts', but reality that affects people. The tree symbolizes the power to define good and evil, but in an independent way, divorced from relationship. The couple had full access to God: they walked in the garden with God, they could ask any question they wanted. They were given immense dignity and freedom, and asked to respect the freedom of the other, God, and the way in which God's self contributed to the relationship. The temptation the tree offered was independence, rather than interdependence. Instead of learning right from wrong within relationships, they would do so independently; instead of right and wrong, good and evil, being relational categories, they became something external you could grasp, take, manipulate, something to be known, rather than something to be lived; instead of going to God to help them discern right from wrong, the humans would make the rules for themselves.

The two humans are tempted to be something they are not, to seek to be God, rather than themselves. And the results are – catastrophic. The harmonious world of equality and interdependence crumbles. Instead of being comfortable and confident in who they are, they now hide, first from one another, by making clothes, then from God. Blame replaces co-operation as the man blames both God ('the woman *you* gave me') and the woman ('*she* gave me the fruit'), as if he had not been a willing participant, and the woman blames the serpent, as if she had not known what she was doing. God's speech exposes the consequences of their actions. The serpent is cursed directly by God, and the ground is cursed, indirectly, by human actions. The humans are not cursed, but will suffer the consequences of their choices.

These consequences affect every relationship. The enmity between the woman and the serpent signals a breakdown of the idyllic picture of interdependence with and care for creation. The words to the woman indicate the breakdown of interpersonal relationships, with 'your desire shall be for your husband, and he shall rule over you'. For the first time, hierarchy and inequality emerge between human beings, as a result or product of sin (not as a command from God). As human beings seek to decide good and evil for themselves, they move away from the radical equality and dignity of creation. God's words to the woman, that he would increase her pains/distress and pregnancies (not 'pain of childbirth', as is often mistranslated) may be seen negatively, but could also be a countermeasure: as the world becomes a much harsher place, an increase in fertility will enable larger families to work a more difficult ground, and it responds to the increased risk of pregnancy loss and child mortality.

God's words to the man are equally weighted in 3.17–19, 'cursed is the ground because of you', and reinforce the breakdown of relationship between human beings and creation. No longer does creation provide easily for human need. Instead, hard work only will bring out what is required. Somehow the humans' distorted aspirations for themselves yield a distorted relationship to nature, as nature becomes something to be tamed and conquered – and, as we are all too aware today, abused. A note of the original inter-dependence of creation sounds with the reminder of the ground creature's formation out of the dust of the earth. The humans belong together, yet their rightful relationship has been disturbed. As soon as God finishes speaking, the man takes over; before they ate the fruit, the woman had been free to speak, and initiated conversa-tion with the serpent. After this, she speaks only once in chapter 3, second, in response to God's question, and falls silent. Now the man speaks, and, in a chilling echo of his naming of the animals in 2.20, he now names his wife, Eve, in the first act illustrating the dramatic consequences of their choices on equality. From then on, he himself will bear the name Adam, rather than be 'the adam', the earth creature', and will claim for himself the whole of what it is to be human. The story of chapter 3 highlights the propensity of human beings to claim more than they are entitled to, an identity at odds with the truth of their place in the world.

Genesis 3 and justice

Genesis 3 is often called 'the Fall', but to regard it as a distinct one-time event obscures its meaning: every human being is invited to see themselves within that story, to recognize it as the story of the human condition, a story that every person participates in in multiple ways.

The individualization of ethics

First, the story diagnoses one of the central problems the world faces as a human takeover of ethics: human beings seek to define right and wrong for themselves, rather than through relationship to God. They put themselves at the centre of everything, and very quickly, as the story develops in the Old Testament, this leads to marketized ethics and unbridled individualism as people do 'what is right in their own eyes'. Multiple visions of right and wrong compete, and it becomes increasingly difficult to pinpoint what 'justice' actually is. Without agreement on what the common good might be, human communities lack a centre to unify and structure their life together, and protect each person. The book of Judges, later on in the Old Testament, explores this point in detail. Human beings want to 'do what is right in their own eyes', be judges of right and wrong for themselves, rather than follow 'what is right in God's eyes'. They pursue radical freedom and radical individualism. As they do so, their communal identity starts to fragment and disintegrate, and conflict erupts regularly as competing definitions of right and wrong yield competing interests. And the less agreement there is on a shared framework of ethics, the more complex it becomes to do justice, and to distinguish justice from revenge. Without the creational framework of human dignity and equality, 'justice' easily becomes distorted, abusive or abused for personal gain. In a deeply individualistic world centred on personal freedom to make moral decisions, ironically, it is individual persons who suffer, because there is no agreement on how or why to protect them. Even as human beings seek to do justice, the question becomes, 'What is justice?' Justice for whom? How do we know?

The sins of the father

Second, the Genesis story highlights the continuity of humanity, and the impact of one generation upon the next. Adam and Eve's actions lead to a change in how human beings relate to one another, to God and to the world around them, and this change will be passed down generations. Closeness to God recedes; children are associated with pain; the enmity between the woman and the serpent will pass down to her children (3.14), and the ground will become harder for every human being to till. Genesis 3 has often been used in arguments about 'original sin', sin that passes down from generation to generation. It is not necessarily helpful to think of this mechanically, as if the very nature of human beings had changed. What is helpful is to recognize the impact of one generation on the next: their actions, choices, mistakes and deliberate sin will always affect and shape those to come. Some have talked of this story in terms of original trauma, passed on through every generation, leaving brokenness in its trail. How does a recognition of intergenerational dynamics help us think about justice? How do we weigh personal responsibility alongside influences, pain and brokenness?

This question was always at the forefront of my mind when I worked in the Probation Service. Day after day, I listened to people who were broken. Many of them had also done terrible things. But you couldn't listen to their story, or read it in multiple reports, without a sense that somehow their history had to be part of defining what 'justice' could look like. One of the people I most remember was a young man – we'll call him Michael. He was only 18, just old enough to be in the adult justice system. He already had multiple convictions for car-related crime, drugs and possession of an offensive weapon. As I got to know him, it became clear that he had grown up in a difficult neighbourhood, in a broken home, with violence at home and on the streets. He had certainly made plenty of bad choices. But unpicking his choices together, one fact kept coming up: he thought he had no choice about carrying a weapon, no choice about joining a gang, because if he didn't, he would be a victim of one. Rightly or wrongly, he felt that his ability to defend himself was a question of life and death. I spent hours with him, listening, probing, putting support in place. He could not understand it. Again and again, he questioned my motives, struggling to trust. He was clever, funny and a bit shy. I grew very fond of him, but no matter how much I tried, he simply could not believe that anyone could possibly have his best interests at heart. He was the most alone person I have ever met, and I knew that it was simply a matter of time until he did something terrible, under the justification of survival. He did. He killed another youth, and landed in prison for decades. As I wrote a report for the judge, I pondered again and again, what is justice? If someone has never experienced love, what is their capacity for justice? How do we weigh up responsibility and guilt? And, perhaps more importantly, what could we do about it, as a society? How do we *see* people like Michael, rather than cast them aside and forget about them, in jail? How do you help someone learn to love and be loved? And how did his own actions shape others and their possible futures?

Scripture revisits this theme again and again, with a constant balance between the effect of one generation on the next, and the need for each generation to come to know God for themselves and be responsible for their own choices; it is not an either/or, but a both/and. A frequent formula in the Old Testament proclaims:

> The LORD, the LORD,
> a God merciful and gracious,
> slow to anger,
> and abounding in steadfast love and faithfulness,
> keeping steadfast love for the thousandth generation,
> forgiving iniquity and transgression and sin,
> yet by no means clearing the guilty,
> but visiting the iniquity of the parents
> upon the children
> and the children's children,
> to the third and the fourth generation.
> (Exodus 34.6–7)

The formula asserts the impact of the brokenness of one generation on the next as children often either endure or participate in sin's consequences. The use of 'parents' and 'children' does not have to be strictly literal, but can refer more widely to a community's relationship to the next generation, a family's, a nation's and so on. The formula holds a sense of justice (not clearing the guilty) and how justice often also negatively affects those around the primary offender. Interestingly, this judicial impact is limited to the number of generations alive during the guilty party's lifetime, that is, three or four. Beyond this, descendants are not held responsible for their forefathers' failings, even if consequences are still there. However, the verse does not start with justice or judgement, but with love and grace: those extend to a thousand generations, and proclaim the vast superiority of grace over retribution. In other words, the link between sin and the brokenness of the next generation is neither permanent nor inevitable, but can be conquered and transformed, provided, as we see here, love and justice are held together.

From abundance to scarcity

A third key feature of this passage is the way it highlights a change of framework for humanity, from abundance to scarcity. The original picture was one of co-operation, generosity and abundance, where human beings had all they needed, and shared equally in work, rest and relationship with God. Genesis 3 chronicles the passage into a world where resources become harder to obtain, the earth's bounty diminishes, animals become threat, and human beings jostle for power and status. Scarcity breeds a different imagination: one that believes that we need to compete for resources to survive, that power is necessary and cannot be shared easily. Such an imagination struggles with co-operation, sharing and generosity; it struggles with the idea of grace and tends to prefer just deserts; it is more likely to lead to oppression and exploitation, justified by reference to survival and the need for security. These are the kind of arguments Western countries have used to justify hoarding vaccines and supplies in the pandemic: survival dictates it, and survival is a powerful drive.

This is only one response to scarcity, obviously. Another would be to co-operate and share, to distinguish between practical and social goods, realize that sharing power does not mean a loss, or that love and grace can expand exponentially. Yet such a response often means fighting against the instinct to survive, to make oneself safe, regardless of what happens to others. Our imagination of the world, and whether it is a place of abundance or scarcity, has a profound impact on how we think about justice. My client Michael, whom we met above, operated entirely out of a framework of scarcity – because that was all he had ever known. He thought the entire world was against him. The wider society within which he was born did so too: he had grown up in poverty despite the UK being one of the richest nations on earth; people like him were often represented in films, in the media, as evil, wasteful, lazy or crazy; he was constantly told that he was a problem to be solved, and that he had little, if anything, to contribute. The criminal justice system was organized in ways that increasingly proclaimed that rehabilitation is too expensive, because it involves time spent listening, caring and working with people, and 'justice' became reduced to punishment or protection of the public.

Very easily, an imagination shaped by scarcity constrains and limits our approaches to justice by defining what is 'possible' or 'reasonable' according to the need to survive and keep ourselves safe. The stories of Scripture call us back to an imagination of generosity and abundance, to proclaim confidently a different way of being, even when faced with scarcity. In Genesis 1, this way of being is encapsulated by the Sabbath: no matter what the circumstances are, the people of Israel are expected to follow the Sabbath, to resist the exploitation of people and resources, resist the idea that survival depends on overwork and the hoarding of resources, and keep making space for all to flourish.

Scripture's insistence on justice, most evident in the Prophets, is an insistence that scarcity is never an excuse for oppression and abuse. The victims of injustice in Scripture are consistently portrayed as those who experience actual scarcity, at the hands of those who fear scarcity. A recurrent refrain highlights 'the widow, the orphan and the alien' as those most likely to experience poverty. Poverty has multiple aspects – a lack of security and housing (Isaiah 14.30; 25.4; Amos 8.4), hunger and thirst (Isaiah 32.6–7; 41.7; Ezekiel 16.49), exploitation by rulers and others (Isaiah 29.19; Jeremiah 2.34; 20.13; Ezekiel 18.12), injustice in court (Isaiah 32.7; Jeremiah 5.28; 22.16) and general economic mistreatment (Amos 2.6; 8.6). Yet poverty is never reduced simply to a dearth of physical resources. The three categories (widow, orphan and alien) point to people who were uniquely vulnerable and lacked social power in ancient Israel, and whose condition is permanent: widows and orphans, without a male protector in a patriarchal society, and aliens, who did not belong to ethnic Israel, may have been forced out of their homes, were often disregarded and had fewer rights. It may be worth stopping and wondering how this may work today: single mothers, children in care and refugees, for instance, are all uniquely vulnerable, and despite the welfare system have less access to social capital. The way that certain groups are often portrayed negatively in the media and on social media encourages caricatures, and creates a subtext of scarcity and fear of the other, who, through their own vulnerability, may have a claim on those with more resources. So, for instance, asylum seekers and immigrants are often portrayed in social media as 'coming to take our jobs' – the idea being that there are not enough jobs here, and others who come from outside are a threat to us. This plays on the legitimate grievances of communities that have lost ways of life and traditional skills in an increasingly global society, where manufacturing is outsourced and traditional work that shaped entire communities, like coal mining, disappears. Scarcity is a reality for these communities, who often find that they have lost not just work, but status and value in the public eye. Asylum seekers are then pitted against these communities as if in competition for scant resources, despite the fact that the UK is an incredibly rich country, with enough resources to enable the flourishing of both, while employment statistics show that they are not in competition for the same jobs anyway. The most damaging aspect of public portrayal of both groups is their stigmatization as less valuable to the common good: asylum seekers are caricatured and unfairly caricatured as 'stealing jobs'; from the opposite angle, disaffected communities are branded as racist or backwards, while their fears and pain are ignored. Neither portrayal attends to the vulnerability of either, or listens to their story in ways that enable dialogue and a move towards resolution.

Passages that speak of poverty in the Hebrew Bible consistently highlight vulnerability and powerlessness, and the corresponding oppression, injustice and abuses of power by those who do not share their social positioning. A frequent word to talk about 'the poor' in Hebrew is actually a verb that means 'humiliated/afflicted/ raped'. There is an affective aspect to poverty, one that implies that these people are not treated and cherished as made in the image of God. It is their powerlessness and vulnerability that matter the most – not just the fact that they lack resources, but that the possibilities for them to gain those resources are cut off, and their humanity diminished.

The suffering of the land

Talk of justice, in Scripture, is never reduced to humankind. The whole of creation suffers, not just human generations or specific people groups. Human actions will have increasing impact on the land, an impact that could scarcely have been imagined by the writers of Genesis. Images of the devastation of creation as a result of human sin and greed abound in the Old Testament; some of them are presented as literal punishment for sin, violence or injustice, as with Noah and the flood (Genesis 6), or used by prophets to illustrate the overwhelming impact of sin (a sin often directly linked to injustice), as in Hosea 4.3 or Jeremiah 4.23–28; the New Testament also picks up on the theme, particularly linked to accounts of end times. Yet, even stronger than the theme of devastation, is that of re-creation: salvation, God's intervention, consistently yields a restoration of creation, with glorious imagery, such as that found in Isaiah 35. Salvation is never reduced to moral redemption for human beings, it is a complete renewal of the whole of creation according to the creational ethic of abundance.

At this point in the twenty-first century, the dire warnings and metaphors of the prophets, of a devastated land whose animals have fled, seem to have come true. Greed and competition have propelled the exploitation of the natural world to extremes few could ever have imagined, and the link between the damage of creation and justice, ever present in the prophets, is laid bare in today's context again, as climate change most affects those who have least contributed to it. Genesis encourages a joined-up way of thinking about climate matters: not compartmentalizing, reducing talk of climate change to questions of science and innovation, but talking of the way in which humans inhabit and interact with their environment, and of how their actions affect both the natural world and other human beings. An increasing number of environmental campaigning organizations are shifting from speaking of melting ice caps and disappearing biodiversity, to focusing on climate justice and enabling those most affected to take a lead in how we respond. Young people all over the world, following the lead of Greta Thunberg, are framing protests on climate action around the failures of adults to hand down a healthy environment to their children, and mourning a world disappearing before they have had a chance to know it. Yet climate justice, globally, goes much further, and recognizes that poorer, rural communities in Africa and Asia, communities often much less visible to those countries that are the primary drivers of environmental disaster, feel the impact of climate change first, and most strongly. Their invisibility has often meant less impetus to tackle the change needed, and reinforced dynamics of injustice at global levels. The acceptance of impact on semi-invisible 'others' suggests that human lives are not 'equal' in practice, even when they are claimed to be in words and international agreements.

Namibia, often referred to as the driest country south of the Sahara desert, is home to a large majority of people who depend on agriculture, fishing, forestry and conservation. Over half the population live in rural areas, with little access to electricity. Climate change is accelerating desertification, making life increasingly precarious. In a conversation with Charles, an elderly man who had lived in a village on the edge of the desert for his entire, long life, he told me: 'I can remember when I was a boy, there were trees over there. Now it's sand and dust and nothing but brush. We need the trees for firewood, but there are none left.' Climate change has had a devastating effect on his community. Wood is essential to many small businesses and many daily tasks. Desertification means fewer trees are growing, and for each tree the community uses, the impact is greater than it was 50 years ago, when they grew more abundantly. This leaves Charles and his community in a double bind: if they keep using trees, they contribute to the problem, but if they don't, livelihoods are at risk. Land that can sustain life is becoming more and more precious, and, with it, conflicts are increasing to try and secure it. Yet Charles's life has contributed very little to global warming. He has never had electricity or a car; he walks to get water, and largely eats what he produces. His grandson has left the village to work for an environmental organization that seeks to do two things: first, make the environmental conversation relevant in Namibia itself, so that the people most affected can have a voice in shaping responses locally and devising local training and projects; and, second, lobby on the world stage so that the interdependence of different countries be recognized, and climate change tackled together at international level.

Coming back to Genesis, Charles's dilemma needs to be looked at in terms of justice, of human dignity, of the impact of human beings on one another, but also in terms of the suffering of the land itself, and of its animals. Human beings are encouraged to care for the earth not just because it is good for them as humans, but because the earth and all its life is valuable and good in God's eyes. Jesus famously picks up on this motif when he reminds the disciples of God's care for the lilies of the field and for the sparrows (Matthew 6.25–33) as evidence of his goodness and trustworthiness. The biblical insistence on the interdependence of humanity and nature helps illuminate why talking of justice is so complex at the level of individuals: as soon as you start pulling on a thread to interrogate injustice, connections between human beings, throughout the generations and throughout the world, appear and reveal that all of us are part of systems and patterns bigger than ourselves, over which we often have little control. As such, it is unlikely that any human being, any heroic leader, would be able to solve an issue whose roots are, to go back to Genesis 3, deep within every single human heart. To do justice is, first and foremost, a communal task.

Questions for reflection

1 Try and think of a situation where doing what is right or just is not obvious. What resources do you use to make a decision? Who defines what is just?
2 Watch the news or read the papers for today. How are different people groups represented? Can you see evidence of an

'economy of scarcity'? How might different groups tell their own story?

3 Can you take a product you have recently bought, and trace its journey? How many hands have made it, distributed it, shaped it? How were they each treated?

In search of original justice

Learning to respond in a broken world

Genesis 1 and 2 had painted creation as a place of spontaneous equality and justice deriving from the character of God. In the Genesis 3 world, the question arises, what next? As bonds of interdependence break down and living beings compete for a place in the world, what is the right response? Humanity has wrestled with responding to these breakdowns throughout the centuries – as one can see from ancient philosophers such as Plato, to multiple religious texts throughout the world, to theology, philosophy, politics, sociology . . . The responses are varied, and, often, contradictory or incompatible, rooted in vastly different imaginations and contexts, disagreeing on the type of solution that can be given, on who has a claim or responsibility within these solutions, and on what aspects of injustice and inequality actually need addressing, or, in some cases, justifying.

How are we, as Christians, meant to respond? What does Scripture have to say about our response? Scripture does not give one uniform answer, nor does it define one political philosophy, structure or system of government that would help. Scripture, in other words, does not give party political answers. What it does do is explore how human beings have tried to organize their lives in partnership with God. As we have seen, Scripture speaks primarily through stories, which we are invited to interact with, ponder and allow to question us back. Using stories matters: they remind us that justice is always rooted in specific contexts, times, cultures and people. Stories keep real people, their pain, hurts and limitations, to the fore. There are different courses of action and different dilemmas in different stories, and, when we take them all together, they shape questions and challenges for today.

Scripture is uncompromisingly honest in naming the problems and their consequences. The categories of thought around justice in Scripture are sin, evil, choice, transgenerational trauma and damage, communal responsibility, brokenness and rupture.

Scripture talks of guilt, shame, anger and punishment on the one hand, and mercy, grace, forgiveness and restitution on the other. It is a very different way of speaking from the moral universe of the therapeutic West, where we talk primarily of personal rights and needs. The biblical world is not without nuance – the interaction of sin and guilt with trauma, for instance, helps us think carefully about how we attend to the complex humanity of the characters in the text.

Humanity is not left to deal with injustice alone; at every step God appears as partner, judge and shepherd to people struggling with themselves and the wider world. In Genesis 3, God neither writes the humans off, nor writes off their actions without follow-up. He makes clothes for them, a compassionate act, yet still bars their access to Eden. This pattern of holding people responsible, yet walking with them as they work through the outcomes of their actions shapes the whole of the Old Testament. The consequences may seem harsh, but not to address evil is to fail the next generation – and the next and the next . . . To deal with evil and its unfolding consequences, in the universe of Scripture, is an act of love for an interconnected, interdependent humanity.

Vestiges of justice

How does the picture of a just, harmonious created world interact with the sombre world of Genesis 3 and beyond? Justice is not lost beyond Genesis 3, it is distorted. The imprint of creation still powerfully shapes human conscience and instincts. It is not very difficult to see today: most human beings have an innate sense of justice. As mentioned earlier, toddlers soon learn the words 'it's not fair', while adults often cry out, 'why me?' These questions do not make sense unless we have some idea of what the world should be like, and we believe that justice and fairness are a right that human beings can appeal to. Scripture assumes that this creational imprint is still carried by human beings, in their conscience and inner selves. All human beings, whether they relate to the God of Scripture or not, are expected to have access to and follow basic moral laws; Israel receives much more specific instructions, but the 'nations' are still judged according to general principles of justice. In the New Testament, Paul's letter to the Romans opens with three chapters that take for granted the idea that basic morality and justice are written into creation, and that even those who do not know God have access to a sense of right and wrong, and are accountable for their response:

> They show that what the law requires is written on their hearts, to which their own conscience also bears witness; and their conflicting thoughts will accuse or perhaps excuse them on the day when, according to my gospel, God, through Jesus Christ, will judge the secret thoughts of all.
> (Romans 2.15–16)

The hopefulness of this picture, however, needs tempering with another biblical insight: human instincts and natural revelation are both limited and twisted out of shape, so that discerning what is just becomes increasingly difficult. To get back to the example of a toddler's spontaneous cry of 'it's not fair', one might wonder, what is this about? An inner sense of justice? Or a sign of self-centredness or entitlement? Or a failure to see the bigger picture? With toddlers, 'it's not fair' often has more to do with not getting their way, or a slice of cake, or having to go to bed early. But it is not always that different with adults, though we are better at masking our motivations and offering justifications. If I apply for a job I don't get but really need or want, it is easy to argue 'it's not fair'. 'Fair' here may be about injustice in the process itself, which needs challenging; it may be about a wider unfairness – the difficulty of getting the right job at the right level of skills and pay, the unfairness of unemployment or wealth differentials more widely. But it may also be about a sense of entitlement, that I deserve something more than the unknown others who have also applied, or, like a toddler and an ill-advised snack, I simply have my wishes and desires denied. If our frequent cries of 'it's not fair' were completely rooted in a search for justice, why would we tolerate so much injustice and inequality around us? Inequality seems to be a default setting of human communities, rather than the justice most of us aspire to.

A sense that justice and fairness should exist does not define what justice might actually look like beyond individual cries for a different experience. Human beings have always found it much easier to identify what injustice looks like than to agree on and implement justice, the common good or flourishing. Some of the differences are rooted in sinful behaviour, in the selfishness shaped by a belief in scarcity and the need for competition and unwillingness to extend costly compassion. Many differences, however, are also rooted in the limited nature of humanity. Every human being only inhabits one time and one place in the world. They are only aware of a certain number of factors impinging on a situation. Sometimes, their best efforts to be just lead to unforeseen consequences and unexpected new injustices being committed. Injustice always has a particular shape rooted in context, but the roots are often invisible and connected in ways we simply cannot see. This is not a justification for doing nothing, but a reminder that attempts at being just need to be marked by humility and provisionality. Doing justice is an ongoing process, through which we discover new aspects of both justice and injustice, the need to adjust our behaviours, and parts of ourselves, as individuals or communities, that we would rather ignore. So, for instance, the Covid-19 pandemic has prompted churches everywhere to hold services online. As communities gathered virtually, we came to realize quite how many people had been shut out of physical services, because of inaccessible buildings, physical disabilities or caring responsibilities. Yet at the same time, many other people were suddenly shut out of services when they moved online, because of digital poverty, or because specific disabilities made it much harder to engage virtually. As churches look at a 'new normal', how we attend to the whole people of God is therefore a complex question. To have a camera in the building is not the same as having the entire community gathered together in one mode, sharing the same experience. We cannot go back to the way in which we marginalized entire groups of people; yet we cannot move forward in ways that either exclude new groups of people or imagine that the only fix needed is an additional camera. We have learnt something about ourselves as a church that needs to reach deep into our consciousness and transform not just our practice but our relationships, so that we work *together* to welcome all.

Wisdom, in Scripture, is (among other things) to pursue justice unceasingly, but also to be aware of our own limits and frailties. In other words, it is to hold the pursuit of justice together with the possibility of grace and compassion, for ourselves and those we interact with, or we may find ourselves under the very judgement we visit upon others. This kind of dilemma, of the passion for doing what's right and the risk of being blind to one's own limitations and faults, is addressed most powerfully through parables in Scripture. Parables get people to react passionately, instinctively, to a story; to say, 'Isn't it obvious that the right thing to do is X, Y and Z?' And then, the storyteller goes, 'Isn't this exactly what you do when . . . ', and reveals the ways in which we compartmentalize our lives and our application of justice. A salient example is that of King David, who had taken Bathsheba, another man's wife, for his own, violating her and murdering her husband. Yet David, as king, was passionate about justice (2 Samuel 8.15). It was not fake, or misguided. He really did try to be just in judicial terms, but he compartmentalized his life, and so the prophet Nathan came and ambushed him:

[Nathan] came to [David], and said, 'There were two men in a certain city, one rich and the other poor. The rich man had very many flocks and herds; but the poor man had nothing but one little ewe lamb, which he had bought. He brought it up, and it grew up with him and with his children; it used to eat of his meagre fare, and drink from his cup, and lie in his bosom, and it was like a daughter to him. Now there came a traveller to the rich man, and he was loath to take one of his own flock or herd to prepare for the wayfarer who had come to him, but he took the poor man's lamb, and prepared that for the guest who had come to him.' Then David's anger was greatly kindled against the man. He said to Nathan, 'As the LORD lives, the man who has done this deserves to die; he shall restore the lamb fourfold, because he did this thing, and because he had no pity.'

Nathan said to David, 'You are the man!'
(2 Samuel 12.1–7)

It is quite easy to identify obvious fault lines in other people's lives, and particularly important to do so when they are leaders with immense influence. Numerous recent scandals surrounding historical figures and respected leaders have highlighted precisely these dynamics. Philanthropists who sustained charity work and justice in many ways nevertheless supported, and even gained the wealth they then shared from the proceeds of, slavery. Statues recently torn down include the one in Bristol of Edward Colston, who made his fortune transporting up to 80,000 slaves from Africa to America in the seventeenth century, but for a long time was honoured for the money he bequeathed various charities. In the same way, churches of all denominations have been rocked by the revelation that some religious leaders who preached love, justice and peace sexually abused men and women behind closed doors. We need people like the prophet Nathan to stand up, point to the disjunction and call for true justice.

Yet Scripture goes one step further: it paints this type of com-partmentalized thinking as part of the human condition. It may be more obvious, and far more damaging, in some, but it is some-thing all of us fall into, and often wish to deny, as Jesus memorably pointed out:

Do not judge, so that you may not be judged. For with the judgement you make you will be judged, and the measure you give will be the measure you get. Why do you see the speck in your neighbour's eye, but do not notice the log in your own eye? Or how can you say to your neighbour, 'Let me take the speck out of your eye', while the log is in your own eye? You hypocrite, first take the log out of your own eye, and then you will see clearly to take the speck out of your neighbour's eye.
(Matthew 7.1–5)

I am passionate about justice. I often rail against the various forms of human slavery at work in the contemporary world, slavery we benefit from in Western nations through cheap products made by people paid a pittance in countries far enough away that we do not see them. And so I research the provenance of some of the things I buy, try to buy fairtrade or ethical products as much as I can afford. And that is quite right, and good. But my passion for justice is full of holes. It doesn't quite extend to refraining from purchasing from certain retailers I love. I still buy products I know I shouldn't because of convenience or laziness. If I am honest, I probably buy more products I should not than products I should. My generosity and willingness to share have limits. I am part of a much wider system of global trade that I cannot control or really influence, which means that, even with the best of intentions, I cannot avoid contributing to the exploitation of others in some ways. The complexity of doing justice brings together my own limitations, my own wrong choices and selfishness, and a whole host of interconnections that I am part of simply by having been born where I was, and living where I do. Acknowledging the complexity of doing justice in an interconnected world can lead to despair, but it is vital: it helps us locate our humanity on a bigger canvas, and acknowledge what we cannot do. It is an antidote against trying to turn ourselves into God. Human beings on their own cannot save the world: we need one another, and we need divine wisdom and help. Recognizing our own frailty then shapes how we call others to do justice – a call that is inescapable once we realize our own enmeshment in structures of injustice.

This enmeshment, this interconnectedness brings us right back to a central insight of Genesis 3: justice is always part of a story. It cannot be abstracted from real people and real lives. Injustice has a human face, and answers to the pain of injustice need to be part of the story of a community, to understand its imagination, its traditions, its deep roots and lofty aspirations.

Justice in Scripture

Scripture holds many stories, interwoven and connected. It talks of 'justice' using the words of different cultures, embedded in different stories over many centuries. We cannot understand the concepts unless we attend to the stories that animate them. Using the word 'justice' in English is therefore a shortcut that translates words heavy with meaning and background. In the Hebrew Bible, words around justice usually occur with other words that appear repeatedly with them, like constant companions. The most common are *mishpat* and *tsedaqah*, often translated as justice and righteousness (e.g. Genesis 18.19; 2 Samuel 8.15; 1 Kings 10.9). *Mishpat* comes from the word for judging, it has judicial connotations and is often used in the context of courts and judgement. But more widely, it is about putting things right, intervening in an unjust situation and fixing it, which can be via a judicial system, but can have a much wider application and apply to actions to deliver the poor or vulnerable or make right some wrong. It is an active kind of word, one that prompts action. *Tsedaqah*, in contrast, is often translated 'right-eousness', but the word isn't very helpful, given it isn't an everyday word! It refers to something being straight, right, in accordance with a norm; when applied to people, it implies something deeply relational, conformity to the demands of a situation or the right configuration of a relationship; it is an inherently communal word. That the two words so often appear together suggests that one requires the other: you need a vision of what is right in order to act and restore justice; and you cannot achieve right relationships or right order unless you do what needs to be done. Together, they point to both commitment and vision in relational and social terms. They are routinely applied to God's actions and his expectations of human beings. Singly or together, the words also often occur linked to others: *hesed*, for steadfast love or loving kindness (Psalm 36.10; 89.14; Hosea 10.12; Micah 6.8), compassion and mercy (Psalm 103; Isaiah 30.18) and love (Deuteronomy 10.18–19) as attributes of God to be reflected in human actions. Justice, therefore, is consist-ently allied with love, grace and compassion. The association is so strong that Rabbi Jonathan Sacks argues that *tsedaqah* inherently combines the ideas of charity and justice (Sacks, 2002, p. 113). In Jewish theology, according to Sacks, justice has to include charity, because nothing in the world belongs to us. Land belongs to God, and is given to human beings in trust. To hoard resources is therefore to hoard what does not belong to us, but must rightfully, justly, be shared with those in need. Justice and righteousness are rooted in the picture of creational harmony, of interdependence and care, of the abundance of creation which precludes the need or right to claim more than one's fair share.

The New Testament's use of 'justice' is deeply rooted in the Old; justice and righteousness again appear as a pair, translating *dikaiosunē* and *krisis*. Justice is as prominent in the New Testament as the Old, and equally refers to God's own righteousness, and the quality of people who live justly. In line with the Old Testament, Jesus blesses those who 'hunger for righteousness' (Matthew 5.6), which more probably refers to overall relational and communal justice than simply to personal discipleship, and he criticizes religious leaders obsessed with the law and rituals but who forget justice and mercy, in echoes of prophetic literature.

In both Old and New Testaments, what is striking is the consistent rooting of justice and righteousness within the character of God, and the corresponding call for human beings to follow in God's footsteps. To be made in God's image is demanding: it puts an ethical claim on us. When we fail to seek justice, we distort the image of God within us, and we ignore the image of God within those who are hurt and oppressed. Pursuing justice means being who we are called to be, by discerning where God is at work, and joining in. And this, in turn, is the 'true worship' that the prophets speak of.

Questions for reflection

1 When was the last time you thought, 'That's not fair!' Exactly what was unfair? How could it be put right? What might another person involved say?
2 What is your 'comfort zone' when it comes to 'doing justice'? What feels challenging or too big? Is there anything you would rather ignore?
3 What do your use of money and buying choices say about your priorities when it comes to justice?

Prayer

Creator God, who imbued the world with your generosity and abundance, we pray that you would open our eyes to see you at work, open our hearts to receive your gifts, including the gift of one another, and open our hands, that we may play our part in tending your creation, in working for justice and redressing the wrongs that maim and hurt the world and its people.

Jesus Christ, who came to proclaim good news to the poor, the prisoners, and the sick, we pray that you would help us hear and respond to your call; that you would show us the riches we already have, and reveal our poverty of imagination and generosity; we pray that you would free us from the need to compete, to hoard resources and to diminish the other, and you would heal us from the wounds of the past, wounds we have inflicted and wounds that have been inflicted on us that we may be released into fullness of life.

Spirit of all truth, who brooded over the waters of creation, we pray that you would reveal to us the truth of our lives, their beauty and their holiness, their sin, brokenness and shadows; we pray that you would sanctify us in our thoughts and in our deeds, that we may love you and our neighbour more deeply, and work with you for the renewal of creation. Amen.

2

From bondage to freedom

Exodus and liberation stories

The first set of texts we looked at in an examination of justice in Scripture were those around creation: texts that proclaimed a positive, constructive view of God, and of the human beings made in God's own image. These texts give a broad-brush account of what lies underneath the world we inhabit: divine gift, abundance and generosity; a deep valuing of human beings, their dignity and fundamental equality; the interdependence of people and creation, and the preciousness of the natural world. And, together with all these, a clarion call for humanity to mirror the divine nature.

From then on, things break down, and the pattern initiated in Genesis 3 picks up speed as conflict, injustice and violence spread, and human beings struggle to walk with God and to live well in a broken world. The shape of brokenness evolves and varies in the many stories of Genesis. Finally, at the end of the book, the people of Israel (the Hebrews) have settled in Egypt, displaced by famine, and rely on the protection of a high-placed relative, Joseph, right-hand man to Pharaoh. The story paves the way for Exodus, a book that shapes the rest of Scripture, and has fired religious and political imagination ever since. It is a book written on a broad canvas, a cosmic story of the battle of good against evil, and a classic story of dramatic liberation of an oppressed people. The people of Israel, once their protector had died and years had passed so their privileged status diminished and was forgotten, find themselves as aliens in a strange land, vulnerable and despised, reduced to slavery and dehumanizing conditions. The story of their liberation captures the imagination, as God musters the whole of creation through plagues on Egypt to convince evil Pharaoh to 'let my people go', then dramatically parts the Sea, and reveals himself spectacularly at Sinai. No wonder Exodus has inspired graphic representations in Hollywood, excited Sunday school retellings, and formed the backbone of entire theological movements that sought to recapture the centrality of justice and liberation so obvious in Exodus.

Exodus 1: Inequality, injustice and violence

Key text: Exodus 1.8–22

Exodus 1 sets the scene with swift, concise and chilling precision. One political actor, Joseph, had invited an entire people group, 'the descendants of Jacob', to come and settle in this new country. Visibly different in culture, ethnicity and religion, they are called 'the Hebrews' by their Egyptian neighbours. They kept their community slightly separate. But politicians come and go, and when Joseph went, others forgot about him and the promises he made. The story highlights the development of institutional prejudice and discrimination incisively. First, rumours are spread, to incite fear – 'The Hebrews are getting too numerous, soon they will be more powerful than us!' The rumours subtly but surely create a 'them and us' divide, with the insinuation that 'they', the Hebrews, will join with Egypt's enemies. There is no proof that this is the case, it is merely fear-mongering that increases the perceived otherness of the Hebrews (1.10). Yet at the same time the Egyptians recognize they need the Hebrews, and so devise ways of tying them to Egypt while exploiting them ever more cheaply. They are turned into slaves, and their otherness is used to justify this differential treatment. When the Hebrews' spirit is not broken by oppression, fear turns to 'dread' (1.12). The rulers capture the imagination of Egypt through fear, and reinforce their control through structural means, through overseers and the supervision of labour. When fear reaches its climax, it is only a short step for Pharaoh to move from oppression to extermination, and he orders the death of all male children: the tactic gets rid of potential troublemakers, those who may one day become a threat, and condemns the people to extinction. Under the new rules, Hebrew girls growing up will either have no mate or be forced to assimilate. The implications of the policy for women are chilling. The sequence of lies, fear and discrimination is not dissimilar to language around migrants, refugees and displaced people today.

The story graphically explores justice and injustice. First, a strong relationship is evidenced between inequality and injustice. The two concepts are not identical, but they are closely related. Defining the Hebrews as 'other', as different, facilitates their unequal and oppressive treatment. The diversity of creation, positive in Genesis 1, has now turned into a pretext for hierarchy and devaluing.

Second, the text shrewdly exposes the power of words and imagination: the public representation of a group shapes how an entire country relates to them. There are exceptions, of course, but the shaping of public imagination is a key feature of oppression here, and highlights how leaders can manipulate an entire people to stay silent in the face of horrendous abuse. This is what Hitler did while enacting the Holocaust; it is how we are often conditioned, today, to ignore the devastating fate of those fleeing war in flimsy boats across the Mediterranean, or even put rules in place to prevent sea rescues of capsizing migrant boats. In both cases, Jews, or refugees, are cast as other, as dangerous, as threatening. Refugees are called 'migrants', so that language hides the fact that they are not moving out of choice, but out of desperation. The division of humanity between self and other prevents the meeting of real people; instead of seeing a fellow human being oppressed next to them, the Egyptians see a *Hebrew* being oppressed, and nationalistic loyalty mixed with fear of difference masks their common humanity and prevents compassion. The Egyptians themselves are also reduced in their humanity, they become caricatures, so that readers expect all Egyptians to be oppressors, and are less likely to be open to Egyptian characters. Both oppressors and oppressed are dehumanized.

Third, Exodus, well ahead of its time, comments on structural or institutional discrimination. As Hebrews are ostracized from positions of power after Joseph, no one defends their interests to Pharaoh. Pharaoh then enshrines discrimination within the political and economic fabric of Egypt. The attention to structural aspects of oppression highlights the abuse of power as a central factor in injustice. The imbalance of power between Pharaoh and the Hebrews is what enables their enslavement to be carried out.

Pharaoh wields enormous structural might, and uses it both to oppress directly and to reinforce the imbalance further by diminishing the social standing of the Hebrews and cutting them off from human solidarity with their Egyptian neighbours. Pharaoh's power enables him to enhance the breakdown of relationship between human beings characteristic of the impact of sin, and misuses the power of the state, normally the guarantor of justice, to enforce injustice.

Fourth, another feature of injustice here is exploitation. That is, the people who lack everything, who are the poorest of the land, are the very people who produce what their oppressors need – palaces and cities. This motif will be taken up again in the prophets as a particularly scandalous aspect of oppression (cf. Jeremiah 22.13–17; Amos 5.11–12). In contrast to Genesis' picture of abundance and Sabbath, now productivity is the final word, and even the post-Genesis 3 hardness of tilling the earth is perverted into heavy toil that benefits others, rather than enables dignity and provision for workers.

Finally, Exodus affirms the importance of the body; the practical plight of the Hebrews matters; the way their bodies are co-opted into Pharaoh's building projects matters. The physical tasks and their toll are stressed repeatedly, bodies define who lives and who dies (baby boys or baby girls), the strength of Hebrew women's bodies in birth is used to shield their children. Bodies need to be seen and recognized for the shape, depth and impact of oppression to be named. At the same time, the text stresses that oppression and discrimination affect more than bodies and social positioning: it is the Hebrews' humanity, ultimately, their very life, that is at stake.

Exodus 1 therefore highlights the social and communal nature of injustice, and pinpoints the responsibility of both leaders and wider community. Pharaoh manipulates the public imagination, but the people of Egypt do have choices, exemplified as the story unfolds by his own daughter's choice to defy his orders and rescue baby Moses. It is the conjunction of a leader with evil intent, and a people ready and keen to see themselves as special and threatened, that makes the conditions for oppression, violence and genocide possible. Violence permeates the account. Violence, in biblical texts, is usually associated with an imbalance of power, including institutional and systemic power (Lynch, 2020, p. 58). Wisdom literature such as Job, Psalms and Proverbs makes a consistent link between violence and injustice. Physical violence is used in enforcing injustice, but more crucially, words, plans and the representation of reality all feed into it; to think violent thoughts, to plot injustice and to nurture the type of imagination that yields injustice is to do violence and harm the other already. The heart and mind are consistently portrayed as the source of evil, with human desire and fear as twin drivers of justice and oppression. The logic of oppression, however, carries within it the seeds of its own destruction: if Pharaoh is ready to dehumanise the Hebrews to ensure his own personal gain, how long before he widens the net? If a people's imagination is shaped in such a way that some human lives are considered expendable, what might they be ready to do to one another? How does such thinking erode the capacity for morality?

Frederick Douglass, an American writer, abolitionist and social reformer, himself a former slave, pondered the fundamental fragility of any system built on the denial of another's humanity: 'Where justice is denied, where poverty is enforced, where ignorance prevails, and where any one class is made to feel that society is an organized conspiracy to oppress, rob and degrade them, neither persons nor property will be safe.' Douglass's insight is not that oppression legitimates violence, but rather, where a leader thinks nothing of sacrificing the lives and well-being of an entire group of people, it will be only a short step to defining the lives of anyone or anything that stands in their way as expendable. The rest of the story of Exodus will unpack this insight, as Pharaoh shows himself willing to sacrifice everything – crops, resources and, ultimately, his own people, to shore up his crumbling position.

Questions for reflection

1 Are there any groups you can identify whose identity is shaped as 'other' in public imagination around you?

2 What power do you personally have in terms of shaping what other people think, and how they are treated? What about the different systems that you are part of, at work, at church, in the family?

3 When have you felt 'other', or invisible? How does this experience shape your understanding of justice?

God's response: Hearing, seeing, acting

After a long time the king of Egypt died. The Israelites groaned under their slavery, and cried out. Out of the slavery their cry for help rose up to God. God heard their groaning, and God remembered his covenant with Abraham, Isaac, and Jacob. God looked upon the Israelites, and God took notice of them. (Exodus 2.23–25)

Then the LORD said, 'I have observed the misery of my people who are in Egypt; I have heard their cry on account of their taskmasters. Indeed, I know their sufferings, and I have come down to deliver them from the Egyptians, and to bring them up out of that land to a good and broad land, a land flowing with milk and honey.
(Exodus 3.7–8)

God hears, God remembers, God sees

The story is told through the eyes of the people of Israel. It is not a dispassionate story, narrated by a 'neutral' observer. It is an involved, caring, personal story. It is told sparsely, and does not try to be comprehensive, look at every point of view, or avoid moral judgement. It is a story that begs readers and listeners to enter into the world of the Hebrews, see their faces and suffer with them. As a story of justice, it proclaims vividly that the place to start is with real people, with the reality of oppression for human lives and bodies. Most powerfully of all, it is a story that says that justice starts with listening and being moved to compassion.

The turning point comes at the end of chapter 2, as the Israelites groaned and cried out. There is no mention of them crying out *to* anyone. They just groan and cry out under the weight of their distress, an inchoate cry of pain and suffering. This is important, because it shows God responding not to a request, but to pain in and of itself. The simple reality of oppression is enough to move

God to action. God's response is rooted in compassion and grace, rather than a legalistic appraisal of right and wrong. The people are suffering, God responds. God hearing the people's cry is enough to put a claim on God: as God hears, God remembers, and God is bound by his own promise to humanity, to act. The suffering of others puts a claim on bystanders. 'God remembered' may suggest that God had forgotten. While on the one hand, of course, we know that God does not forget, and as the story develops, it is clear that God's hand had been over Moses before the people cried out, the story nevertheless is faithful to the lived experience of people in slavery. From their perspective, God had forgotten. Suffering often traps the sufferer into a reality that cuts them off from others, where they feel isolated and misunderstood. At the height of the war in Syria, I asked a Syrian friend of mine how our church could pray. She said, 'We want to know that people care. We're alone, the world has forgotten us. Syria was a birthplace of Christianity, and Christians are disappearing. There is almost no one left. No one cares.' Regardless of how many of us actually cared, the lived reality for her, and many others, was that practically, in everyday life, they were forgotten.

In Exodus, it is not the people's responsibility to break down the wall created by their suffering, it is God's responsibility, as the outside party. The rest of the story shows quite how much work it takes for God to be heard, seen and trusted by a people whose entire experience told them they were alone, and the world – and possibly God – was against them.

God hears, God remembers, then God sees and takes notice (Exodus 2.25). The Hebrew word translated as 'take notice' actually goes further; it says, 'God *knew*'. Seeing leads to recognition and understanding. This is repeated in God's speech to Moses in 3.7: 'I *know* their sufferings.' God enters the lived reality of the Israelites; God does not simply note it, as an interesting fact or testimony in a judicial process. God does not just know what happened, he knows *their sufferings*. This knowledge then prompts God to action, action anchored in relational dynamics: it is about listening, seeing, knowing, all of which imply a direct relationship with the suffering ones. When God acts, this dynamic is preserved: God works with Moses, Aaron and the people. God could easily have spoken to Pharaoh directly, or moved the people out. Instead, God involved the people. First, he witnesses to their suffering. Then God names the reality of oppression, and confronts the oppressor with the truth. At every step, God acts in complete opposition to Pharaoh, treating the people as covenant partners and listening to their voices, moved to a compassion Pharaoh cannot summon. In so doing, God affirms their humanity and dignity, and challenges the politics of Egypt. Pharaoh cannot afford compassion, because compassion would undermine the very possibility of building a hierarchical empire designed to benefit the few at the expense of the many. Compassion and empire are mutually exclusive. Instead, compassion is a motivator for justice, because it seeks the good of the other, to build conditions of living that enable the flourishing of all. The uniting of compassion and justice is what enables justice to address the whole person, their dignity and worth.

Exodus has inspired countless generations of activists and reformers. Liberation Theology, a branch of theology focused on justice, stresses repeatedly that the proper starting point in thinking about justice is not concepts but people, their experience, and what can be done in response. It seeks to understand how unjust practices are sustained, how they can be challenged, and how those very people, often treated as non-human, can reshape, challenge and correct the distortions that have led to gross injustice. As such, doing justice is always relational, and has to be shaped by the very people who know what it is to be treated unjustly.

The temptation, from the outside, is always to work *for* others, rather than *with* others. To explore justice with others is more difficult, complex and challenging: it forces us to realize how our own position shapes our imagination of what is possible or desirable; it forces us to attend to the other, their aspirations and needs, and seek to build a better world together, which, necessarily, will be different from the world we imagine for ourselves only. It also forces the 'outsiders' to see themselves as the 'other' and voluntarily yield the centre ground to those who will define the path ahead. 'Working *with*' challenges all involved to let go of being the defining centre themselves and truly explore what they can hold and build in common.

Working *with* is hard work – the entire way Western societies are structured assumes that the privileged, or those in power, will solve the problem of those they consider poor or powerless or problematic, through programmes, welfare or giving to charities. When I became a probation officer, I unconsciously brought this mindset with me, and the 'system' encouraged it: we were expected to set up education opportunities, solve housing problems, improve access to employment, assess mental health issues, and so on, for offenders. All of this was good, except that it treated offenders as objects of 'interventions', and often the interventions failed. They were interventions designed by those who could not comprehend the mindset, imagination or life experience of those whose lives they tried to change. Remember Michael, the young man I introduced in Chapter 1? Trying to arrange education, employment or better housing was simply irrelevant to him. To a middle-class professional, they looked like the right issues to help him gain a stake in society, self-esteem, dignity. And of course, they are crucial. But to him, at this point, they were distractions from the desperate need to survive that gnawed at him, the fear of being attacked that was always present. They were yet another set of things done to him by a society that kept making him feel worthless and unloved.

Working *with* Michael was a challenge. He was combative and aggressive, and could not see how anyone who had not lived the life he lived could possibly help. Both he and I needed to move towards each other, and allow the other to challenge how we viewed the world. I spent more time listening, less time 'intervening' (though doing so was against the 'national targets' set for my limited time with him). We built up a relationship, one where he puzzled about why I would even want to spend time with him, and where I tried to listen to all the hurt and trauma that he tried to hide. In the midst of it, I discovered his sense of humour, his incisive understanding of politics and society, and a lost, unloved boy. What would it mean to build rehabilitation services by listening to people like Michael, and negotiating their needs with those of wider society?

Exodus however goes further, and makes the extraordinary claim that God himself chooses to work in this way: to listen, to hear, to see, to know, to act in partnership. The world is never back to the way God had designed it, or exactly how God seeks to shape it: it is always shaped just as strongly by human instincts, frailties and brokenness. Laws are not ideal, but shaped to be culturally appropriate for humans whose imagination is bound by time and place. The Old Testament explores the art of the possible, rather than seeks to impose an ideal. The result is an extraordinary, moving and, at times, frustrating partnership, and a story of the deepest grace, one that will continue in the New Testament – the early Church is still on a journey with God to find shapes of life that honour God and one another.

Justice and judgement

Telling the story from within the people's experience, and chronicling how God enters into and transforms that experience, is at the heart of Exodus. Readers are drawn in too, and instinctively decide that something must be done. To decide that something must be done, to label a situation 'unjust', is to make a judgement. Justice inevitably involves value assessments and judgements, before any remedial action can be taken, and judgements imply a frame of reference that claims that certain situations are normative, while others are aberrant. In other words, to judge a situation as unjust means we have a picture of what would be just, and we are affirming that this picture is true and normative and must prevail over all, regardless of whether they agree with this norm.

This is where people start to differ and argue. Who gets to decide what is just? What criteria do you use? Whose perspectives do you take into account? If, for instance, you believe, as many ancient cultures did, that the world has been ordered in such a way that rulers and kings have more power, with each strata of society ordained to its proper place, then slavery and inequality are part of what is just and necessary for a thriving society. If you believe that society should be ordered according to merit and gift, and that hard work is the primary driver of social positioning, the shape of justice and liberation will be rather different: you may seek to establish equality of opportunity between different groups, but not worry quite so much about inequality of outcome. Furthermore, there is a question regarding clashes between different value bases within a society: a value system is needed for justice to be shaped, yet competing views on justice make this difficult. All may agree that murder is wrong (clearly, in Exodus, both Hebrews and Egyptians considered murder problematic), but what about less tangible questions, those that cannot be codified in a legal system, the kind of values that shape informal interactions, economic priorities, what we teach in schools? How does power and who holds it shape what values different groups hold? The root question is, what shapes our imagination, as individuals and communities?

In Exodus, imagination is shaped by divine action. The judgement visited on Egypt through the plagues roots the story in creation. The plagues are a cosmic, rather than judicial, action, as God musters the forces of nature in a public judgement on Egypt's offences. The public nature of the judgement matters, in that justice involves bearing witness to the truth of a situation, proclaiming what should be different, and thereby shaping or reshaping the public imagination. Here, the plagues proclaim that oppression, ruthlessness, cruelty and the misuse of power are wrong, and those responsible will be held to account. It is judgement, a pronouncement, that none can ignore. It is also a direct challenge to the way the Egyptians understand creation and life. It challenges the idea that Pharaoh is divine. It challenges narratives of gods linked to different natural phenomena. It challenges a culture within which nature had become exploited by a Pharaoh willing to sacrifice animals and crops as well as humans. The Sabbath principle, central to divine creation in Genesis, stands in direct opposition to the Egyptian relationship to the world and its people. A nation marked by relentless hard work and productivity is forced to a halt by the God of heaven and earth.

To pass judgement on a situation and claim it is unjust is there-fore a profoundly political act, because it claims a narrative of truth about how the world should be, with consequences for how human lives and societies are to be shaped. In Exodus, to seek justice means breaking down the power of Pharaoh, and undermining the foundations of dehumanizing, ethnically based enslavement. To seek justice is never politically neutral, yet neither is it tied to any particular system, party or philosophy. Every country in the world has those who work towards justice in multiple areas; some may do better than others, but neither in Scripture nor in the world as we know it do we ever see a perfectly just society. Justice is an ongoing task of learning and responding.

Scripture itself casts doubt on the idea that a system could ever be the answer to the problem of injustice. The Old Testament explores a variety of political systems – councils of elders, kings, military leaders, religious leadership, leaders chosen by the people, leaders chosen by representatives, leaders emerging from the people, leaders who inherit their position. The trials and tribulations of Israel as a political entity are chronicled through Joshua to 2 Kings. Systems that are inherently abusive, such as ones resting on slavery, or systems that promote the hoarding of resources by a centralized hierarchical leader, are condemned. However, the variety of political structures is linked by one dominant thread: the dangers of power and abusing it, and the roots of abuse and injustice, not primarily in systems, but in the human heart of leaders and the people who enable their leadership to thrive. Hence in every configuration of political systems, we find stories of those fighting for justice, stories of injustice and abuse, and stories of human–divine partnership in trying to build a better world. Every story of justice has political import, but none is party political. They are primarily prophetic stories: stories that prompt us to ask questions of ourselves and of what we notice around us, so that we too can hear, see and act.

God's initiative

The framework for judgement in Exodus is firmly rooted within the divine nature, rather than within human constructs and philosophies, or human weighing up of responsibilities and actions. It is God who initiates justice. For as much as the story enables us to see through the people's eyes, the narrator nevertheless leaves clues that show that God started to work for liberation long before the people recognized his presence or cried out. God blessed the midwives who saved Hebrew babies. God prepared Moses uniquely for the task that would be set before him. The story is told in a matter-of-fact way, of baby Moses put in a basket, sent down the Nile and rescued by Pharaoh's daughter. Yet as the threads of the story come together, it becomes clear that it was no accident and that God had been working carefully.

God's initiative shapes the story differently to what it could have been had it rested mostly on human action towards liberation. Moses' birth and upbringing shatter the strict self/other distinction between Hebrews and Egyptians. Moses has a foot in each camp, which enables him to relate to both groups, but also prevents a simplistic divide and caricature. Because Pharaoh's daughter appears, Egyptians are humanized. God's action here challenges the imagination of Egypt and its breaking down of humanity into separate camps. God's initiative gives Egypt a chance; Pharaoh refuses to take it, but that chance is made available, showing God's sovereignty and care for all, not just Israel. To seek justice means to ask questions of the welfare of Egypt too.

God's initiative reaches back to his covenant (Exodus 1.24), which sets justice within a relational and narrative framework. God had made a covenant with Abraham: 'I have chosen him, that he may charge his children and his household after him to keep the way of the LORD by doing righteousness and justice; so that the LORD may bring about for Abraham what he has promised him' (Genesis 18.19). God's promise to Abraham was a promise with an underlying purpose, to do justice and righteousness. When God refers back to his covenant, it sets his action of liberation within this much wider arc – liberation is not an end point, but a step within the bigger story of setting aside a people whose way of life will be a proclamation of justice and righteousness. The public judgement on Egypt is part of this framework, teaching not just Egypt, but Israel too, how justice needs to be shaped. The people's journey of liberation is one within which they will need freeing from the imagination of Egypt in order to enter fully into a new way of living.

Questions for reflection

1 What can you see around you that speaks of justice and injustice? How comfortable do you feel making a judgement on what is just or not?

2 There is a project in 50 countries called 'The Human Library'. Instead of books, you can borrow a person you would not normally meet and listen to their story. Who might you 'borrow' and why? How might seeing and hearing their story change you?

3 God's response is first and foremost one of compassion for his suffering people; who do you feel instinctive compassion for? How could you help others share in this?

Transforming people

Everything so far points to the liberation of the people as an event of cosmic importance, meant to challenge the imagination and practices of all involved. As the story proceeds, the discomfort of this challenge is brought out clearly in the interactions between Pharaoh, Moses and the people of Israel.

Pharaoh: a threatened leader

Key text: Exodus 5.1–14

Pharaoh is the individual character most obviously challenged in this story. He embodies Egypt and all its practices; he is painted as responsible for Israel and Egypt's woes, though it is clear from the text that his officials – his army, employees and Egyptian overseers and taskmasters – support his policies and wholeheartedly implement his commands. The mystique surrounding pharaohs, together with the enormous imbalance of power with the people, contributes to this portrait; however, tyrants need hands and hearts to put their plans into action. It is the interaction of leadership and public imagination that makes sustained, ongoing oppression possible. Pharaoh is held responsible both as leader and as representative of attitudes that many have colluded with.

Moses' words to Pharaoh highlight the nature of the challenge. Moses relays the words of God in the first person, as prophets do – God speaking directly to Pharaoh: 'Thus says the LORD, the God of Israel, "Let my people go, so that they may celebrate a festival to me in the wilderness"' (Exodus 5.1). The words are a command from a higher authority. This would rile Pharaoh. Considered divine, he would expect a god to speak to him directly, not give orders via an intermediary. The method of communication, as well as the tone, is a challenge to Pharaoh's position. Pharaoh's position and representation in Egypt claim a place for him that is beyond what any human being can claim. Just as the two humans in Genesis 2—3 try and grasp what is not theirs, the ability to be like God, Pharaoh has a radically false sense of who he is and what his rightful place may be, and this grasping, mistaken identity is integral to the configuration of injustice and oppression. Seeing himself as intrinsically more worthy than others opens the door to exploitation and a justification for inequality. The challenge is not lost on Pharaoh, as his sneering reply shows, treating the Lord as an unknown, minor and impotent deity he need not fear. Just as Moses had relayed God's message, prefaced with 'Thus says the LORD', with an order to let the people go, the taskmasters tell the Hebrews, 'Thus says Pharaoh' (5.10), and transmit an order for the people to keep working, even harder. The stage is set for a showdown between the Lord of the universe and a pretend god of Egypt.

Moses had not mentioned injustice, oppression or even freedom. He had simply asked for the people to go and celebrate a festival to the Lord in the wilderness. At first reading, this does not seem like such a big ask. However, to celebrate a festival to 'the LORD, the God of Israel', is for Israel to proclaim and mark out its own, separate identity. For a dehumanized, ground-down people, claiming a distinctive identity would be a dangerous thing. It is much easier for Pharaoh to maintain control by assimilating the Hebrews, or disabling their ability to see themselves as one people, and by preventing them from the deeply human action of worshipping in ways that reflect their specific identity and culture. Freedom of religion is a threat to totalitarian systems, because it implies freedom of thought and the ability to imagine a different future that may disrupt the present.

Furthermore, the request implies a cessation of work, a return to the Sabbath principle that says that work and productivity are not ultimate goals. Pharaoh immediately seizes on the economic impact of the request. It is stopping work, even for a short time, that enrages him, and his response centres on work and economics: he imposes more work on the Hebrews, thereby reasserting his own vision of the world. Pharaoh's imagination is constrained; he cannot see a different way forward other than deepening (or hardening) what has been before. Despite increasing evidence that his strategy is not working, and will bring disaster, he keeps going along the same tracks. He redoubles oppression and harshness, repeats the fear-inducing claim that the Hebrews are numerous, and blames them for being 'lazy' (5.8). Once again, Pharaoh demonstrates the features of oppressive leaders throughout history. He constructs a false reality which he uses to shape the public imagination; he hides the level of his own power by claiming others have more than he has (by being more numerous) and blames victims for their plight.

Pharaoh's first response had been 'Who is the LORD, that I should heed him and let Israel go? I do not know the LORD, and I will not let Israel go' (5.2). The series of plagues is repeatedly said to show God's mastery over creation and teach Pharaoh 'so that *you may know* I am the LORD' (7.5, 17; 8.10, 22; 9.14, 29; 11.7; 14.4, 8). Pharaoh, it turns out, did not really want to hear the answer to his own question. The prospect is too frightening: he would not only lose his workforce, but an entire narrative of meaning about how the world works, and his own place within it. Instead of yielding to truth, he tries to shore up his crumbling version of the world through violence. If one steps out of the Hebrew perspective for a minute, it is possible to empathize (a little!) with Pharaoh's plight. He is a product of his society and culture, formed by the traditions and beliefs of Egypt, and his entire world, identity, self-worth and place in society rested on interconnected beliefs about the world and human beings. Listening to Moses would lose him everything he values – though he would gain truth and the opportunity to enable a new, just order. But doing so would mean relinquishing his power, his own mistaken sense of who he is. It would mean embracing compassion, and entering the consciousness and pain of what his behaviour has caused. Fear is a powerful motivator; if our imagination is shaped by a belief in scarcity then letting go of power, status and privilege is frightening.

However, if instead of seeing power and status as finite goods, we saw them as goods to be shared, which increase as we share them, how would this change our attitudes to debates around responses to discrimination in its many forms? Does extending the space at the table, increasing the amount of voices, constitute a loss, or does it enrich the whole? How do we feel about claiming no more and no less than our rightful place in the order of creation, on an equal footing with every other human being? The story of Pharaoh suggests that an imagination shaped by justice needs to start with a reappraisal of the place of the self: Pharaoh needs to see himself as he truly is, one human being among many, interdependent, made in the image of God. It is the human heart, as well as structures, that need to be changed – but Pharaoh's heart is hard, and compassion, threatening.

Ultimately, Pharaoh's refusal to accept truth leads to disaster. He is held responsible, as leader of Egypt, for the suffering of many innocent Egyptian children who die in the final plague. The story is uncomfortable. Did judgement on Egypt necessitate such traumatic events? Why implicate all Egyptians, when they had not all participated in Pharaoh's schemes? There are no clear answers in the text. A cursory look at history books, however, suggests that the story reflects a deep historical truth: tyrants hurt their own people, and bad leaders cause suffering to the most vulnerable, who have often had no part in shaping the world they inhabit. The story is not an idealized version of a world where liberation can happen easily and without cost. It shows that oppression comes in many forms, and oppressive leaders like Pharaoh do not just oppress the 'other', here Israel – their oppression and injustice affect and endanger everyone. Injustice is linked to an entire world view that shapes every corner of a society, affects every person and ripples out in ever-widening circles until no one is safe – not even, it turns out, Pharaoh himself.

The transformation of Moses

Pharaoh likes to think that he stands against God in the battle for the Hebrew slaves. Narratively, however, his character is contrasted to Moses. This Pharaoh succeeded the ruler who had been in power when Moses was born and adopted by his daughter. He and Moses likely had similar educations, and knew each other. Moses meets God through an unusual natural world event, the burning bush. Pharaoh is invited to know God through extraordinary natural events – the plagues. The two men react in opposite ways, even though they share a culture and upbringing.

Moses' unusual childhood set him in an ambiguous position, with a dual heritage, a potential bridge between two cultures. Without his privileged upbringing, he may not have had access to Pharaoh to challenge him and lead the people out. His upbringing, however, shaped his imagination with the mores of Egypt.

> One day, after Moses had grown up, he went out to his people and saw their forced labour. He saw an Egyptian beating a Hebrew, one of his kinsfolk. He looked this way and that, and seeing no one he killed the Egyptian and hid him in the sand. When he went out the next day, he saw two Hebrews fighting; and he said to the one who was in the wrong, 'Why do you strike your fellow Hebrew?' He answered, 'Who made you a ruler and judge over us? Do you mean to kill me as you killed the Egyptian?' Then Moses was afraid and thought, 'Surely the thing is known.' When Pharaoh heard of it, he sought to kill Moses.
> (Exodus 2.11–15)

Just like Pharaoh, and despite the counter example of the woman who raised him, Moses sees the world in binary opposites, with a sharp distinction between Egyptian and Hebrew. The distinction creates expectations that do not reflect reality: when two Hebrews fight, he sees their fighting as qualitatively different from his own fight with the Egyptian. He justifies his own actions because they affected an Egyptian, an 'other' defined as oppressor. He sees his own action within a framework of justice, and those of the two Hebrews as merely a fight, without seeking to understand underlying complexities. He meets neither the Egyptian nor the Hebrews as real people, complex and multifaceted. Labels often work against relationships by clouding real persons and turning them into projections of fears, prejudices and impressions.

Putting people in categories is a natural human tendency; categories, generalizations and patterns enable us to make sense of reality quickly, to know how to relate and behave in different situations without having to start from first principles every time. In animals, we call it instinct or conditioning. A response that becomes ingrained deep within body and mind, based on a combination of past experiences, and, for human beings, the shape of our cultures, families and communities. To have an awareness of the cultural preferences of different national groups we may come into contact with, for instance, is helpful: as a French person, I grew up within a culture where personal information was more freely shared than it is in England, where I now live. My home culture expected a lesser degree of privacy, and withdrawing information or resisting physical contact would be considered rude. Living in England, at first, my openness about feelings, thoughts and personal life could often be misconstrued as oversharing, and what I considered being honest was occasionally considered rude or insensitive. Identifying the patterns of thinking and behaviour that differed between the two cultures was immensely helpful in working out how to relate well, and consciously deciding how to inhabit my dual citizenship. To assume that every French or English person conforms to a precise iteration of these preferences, however, would be unhelpful. When general patterns become fixed and rigid, they quickly slide into fixed stereotypes that prevent people from seeing the other person for who they are. In England, I am often told, 'You're so French!', whereas in France, I am consistently told, 'You're so British!' The two cannot be simultaneously true, and reflect the cultural projections of the speakers, rather than an interaction with me as a person who lives in between cultures.

This tendency takes a sinister turn if entire people groups are stigmatized and caricatured, often in ways that do not reflect even a sliver of truth, and become part of a strategy for control and self-interest, like Pharaoh's characterization of the Hebrews as numerous, dangerous and lazy. Here, Moses' easy categorization of people into oppressors and victims leads him to murder an Egyptian, and fail to engage with the interpersonal dynamics between other Hebrews. Moses' simplistic categorization of people into good and bad prevents him from recognizing that everyone is located within complex configurations of power, where aspects of our lives confer different degrees of influence, status and oppression.

Moses himself is simultaneously privileged (due to his childhood) and part of an oppressed group; he is powerful due to his knowledge and understanding of Egyptian culture and familiarity with its leaders, yet this very aspect of his power makes him suspicious and untrustworthy to his fellow Hebrews, as he is no longer fully 'one of them'. He is powerful as a man in a patriarchal culture, yet his maleness makes him a threat and therefore vulnerable before Pharaoh. As Moses develops, he gradually learns to inhabit his role in Israel and Egypt with more nuance and complexity.

Moses' imagination is shaped by Egypt in other ways, too. His first reaction to injustice is to try and overpower it: he responds to violence with violence, in retributive fashion, with an escalation. Beating is answered with killing. Pharaoh will respond in kind, and seek to kill Moses. The logic of Egypt may dress itself up as justice, but risks sliding into an unending cycle of violence that does not achieve long-term change. Moses also attempts to bring about justice in secret, and illegally – in contrast with the need for justice to bear witness and shape public imagination.

Moses' time in the desert is crucial in enabling him to grow and be shaped as a leader by his early, unsuccessful, engagement with questions of justice. In the desert, he struggles with who he is, and his limitations; he will go from a confident young man who kills an Egyptian and challenges slaves fighting, to a man who doubts he has much to offer, when God sets him the task to lead the people into freedom. He comes up with multiple reasons for his doubt in Exodus 3—4 as God speaks to him in the burning bush. Yet it is this new-found awareness of his limitations and the need to rely on others – God, his brother Aaron, his wife Zipporah – that qualifies him as a leader. Time in the desert was crucial for Moses' imagination to begin to be converted, and for Egypt to lessen its hold. It will take time, however, and the work of converting the imagination carries on throughout his life and into a second, much longer period in the desert, with all the people. A crucial point comes in the key text Exodus 18.13–26.

By then, the people have left Egypt and are wandering the wilderness. Leaving Egypt behind has not instantly solved questions of justice. They may not be slaves any more, but disputes, disagreements and injustices are still part of the daily life of the community, and some form of arbitration is needed. Moses' thinking, however, is still trapped in Egypt. He sits alone, as primary leader, holding all the power and defining justice. He consults with God, but still sets himself up as a little pharaoh. His imagination of community life and social structures simply mirrors that of Egypt. Moses does have a special role, in teaching people the ways of God's justice, but he does not have to do it alone. He must learn to let go of Egypt's autocratic models, disperse leadership and share power. Autocratic leadership is inherently open to abuse, and does not recognize the abilities, skills and gifts of other human beings. A just community is one within which the gifts of all are being recognized and put to the service of the whole, while no one person is over-extended. Moses may have been extraordinarily gifted, but he needs to learn to rein in his reach to make space for others to grow and bring their own unique contributions to the community.

The liberation of the imagination

Moses' and Pharaoh's challenges are replicated at the level of the entire people. Egypt and Israel as a whole are invited to rethink their place in the world and how they relate. Exodus is not simply a story of physical liberation, but a story with a much more fundamental call: the liberation and conversion of the imagination.

The people's struggles with the imagination of Egypt are clear throughout – in their distrust of Moses, their fear of taking steps to move away from what they knew, however bad, their constant looking back to Egypt and wondering whether they should return, and their captivity to the gods of Egypt. Captivity to foreign gods is not an isolated question of religious freedom; throughout the Old Testament, religion is a powerful force that shapes the whole of life. Worship of Yahweh, the covenantal God of Israel, is inescapably bound to social structures sharply at odds with those of Egypt and, later, Canaan. Faith is not politically neutral, but shapes beliefs about worth, equality, justice, rights and responsibilities, which have a profound impact on societies and, in particular, their most vulnerable members. Worship and justice are two sides of the same coin – hence the call to let the people go and worship.

A salient story in reshaping the imagination is that of manna in the desert in the key text Exodus 16.1–8.

The people of Israel have seen the plagues on Egypt, the parting of the waters, a pillar of cloud leading them by day, and a pillar of light by night. But nothing they can *see* is enough to overcome the deep patterns of thought and belief ingrained by life in Egypt. Habit and imagination are more powerful forces than demonstration, proof and new experience.

Experience may enable faith to begin, but true conversion needs the habits of the lifetime, and the deconstruction of previous life and thought patterns. Those working for environmental justice have long been aware that scientific fact, experience of more extreme weather and well-thought-out arguments are not enough to change the cultures and habits of the Western world. Climate change denial does not respond to reasoned argument, though pictures of cute animals might prompt willingness to minimize plastic use. Living unsustainably is so ingrained in the way daily life is organized, in patterns of social organization, work, industry and trade, that to alter attitudes to the environment is an enormous undertaking, one that involves such fundamental changes that often we are content to simply tinker at the edges, or deny the urgency of the task, because it is all we can face. To truly deal with climate change means a collective conversion – one that affects our understanding of our rightful place in the world as human beings, our relationship to one another and how different parts of the world are affected, and questions the philosophies that underlie patterns of consumption, travel, resource use and so on. It would challenge both our sense of freedom and our sense of rights, reconceptualizing freedom as contingent on the freedom and welfare of others – including the natural world – and rights as contingent on our responsibilities to the rest of creation. In other words, it would mean accepting that to be human is to be limited in what we can claim for ourselves, and how we should relate to the world. Following this, we would then need to relearn how to live in sustainable ways, building habits of recycling, of less consumption, of choosing different products, of travelling less and so on. It is the work of a lifetime for individuals, and for entire societies.

This is at the heart of what Israel needs to learn in relation to justice. The people are still held hostage to an imagination of scarcity. Despite the wonders they have witnessed, they are afraid that food will be scarce. Their experience in Egypt has not prepared them to believe that God will provide. The trauma of slavery and oppression has limited their ability to be loved and cherished, limited their sense of worth before God. They may be physically free, but they carry the trauma with them in ways that will again and again affect their ability to form a new, healthy community. The remedy seems harsh – years wandering the desert, in between bondage and freedom, while their imagination and the physical community that derives from it is reshaped. Without undergoing this experience, they would bring the imagination of Egypt into the Promised Land – and risk reproducing the patterns and injustices they have left behind.

The first lesson they learn with manna is that God cares, that they are valuable, that their bodies, exploited and mistreated in slavery, are worth feeding, and worth resting on the Sabbath. They do not have to work for food, to prove they merit or deserve it. God feeds them because they are human, in need, and loved. The provision of manna severs the link between care and merit, and invites Israel to see itself differently. It is an invitation to step into self-esteem and worth. The learning does not stop there, however. Each person is to 'pick their fill'. There is an inherent justice and equality to provision in the desert: no-one is to take more than they need – if they do, it will rot. Such manner of provision is another direct challenge to the economy of Egypt, where a few held vast resources whilst others struggled. Here, in the desert, all are equal before God, and no-one is allowed to hoard resources at the expense of others, or for fear of tomorrow. They plan for the Sabbath day by gathering double, but no-one is allowed to gather more than needed. Each day provides the bread of today – the story looms large behind the words of the Lord's Prayer, 'give us today our daily bread'. This is a lesson in radical justice, and in radical trust. The specific instructions for the Sabbath reset the clock based on the patterns of Creation. They proclaim that there is more to being human than food and work, that human life is more than mere survival. In the desert, a place of utter scarcity, the people are to live in abundance of food, and abundance of rest. If they can do so in the desert, then maybe they will be shaped for a good life in the promised land.

The episode also touches a different part of Israel's imagination – how they relate to leaders. Initially they complain to Moses and Aaron. In the imagination of Egypt, leaders are responsible for everything, including provision of food. In the distribution of manna, each person has to behave responsibly. Israel's leaders are not all-powerful autocrats; Israel has to learn that it is God who provides, and their leaders are not God. A more appropriate vision for leadership emerges, as Moses and Aaron teach the people the ways of God so that they can work together justly. A specific task of leadership emerges towards the end of the passage: Aaron and Moses are to perform actions to help the people remember, by saving some manna and preserving the story behind it. They have a unique responsibility as guardians of the public imagination, holding the stories of the community, and enabling these stories to keep shaping the people for years to come.

Questions for reflection

1 Does Pharaoh's story help us understand why we are sometimes fearful of, or push back against, those who ask for redress in the face of discrimination?
2 Can you think of one habit you might take up that may help you live more justly or sustainably?
3 Who are the guardians of collective imagination today – in society, in local communities, in churches? What stories might you pass on that may shape another generation?

Exodus as a prophetic book

As a story of liberation, Exodus has often been read as looking both backwards and forwards: backwards to what God has done in the past, and forwards to what God may do in similar ways in the present and future. The question is, how do we move from past patterns to present realities? How do we read faithfully, and attend to the shape of oppression and liberation in the story that is told, while being sensitive to the different shape and context of injustice today? Our response needs to draw on Exodus, but can never simply reproduce it. In other words, how do we – and can we – understand Exodus as a model, yet not one to be reproduced exactly?

Exodus is a whole story, with an integrity and shape of its own, but it is not an isolated story. It is part of a bigger one, and of a book that contains a number of other stories that complement, challenge and nuance our reading. To read Exodus well, we need to place it within this bigger framework. We have already considered the many echoes of the creation stories and their definition of right and wrong, and the way in which covenants with Noah and Abraham form a backdrop to God's 'remembering' of Israel in Exodus 2. There is, however, more to the back story of both Egypt and Israel.

The back story

The back story is better known from its popular retelling, Andrew Lloyd Webber and Tim Rice's musical *Joseph and the Amazing Technicolor Dreamcoat*. It is more of a Sunday school-type retelling, with Joseph as a wonderful hero, and disturbing parts of the narrative glossed over (the stunning music really is the point of the show!). The musical traces the story back to the account of Jacob and his sons. Sibling rivalry causes a rift between younger brother Joseph, who has dreams of grandeur, and the rest of his brothers. Joseph's dreams have his brothers and parents bow to him: the picture is deeply consonant with the imagination of Egypt already, with its God-like leader whom all others respect and even worship. Joseph's brothers sell him into slavery and he is taken to Egypt.

Joseph learns much in Egypt; he goes from being a shepherd boy, to Pharaoh's trusted right arm. When famine threatens, Joseph plans well, and during years of abundance, he accumulates food to resource years of scarcity. His careful management brings his brothers to Egypt to look for food and to enable a touching family reunion. When his brothers and father (but not his mother, who has died) are reunited with him, together they all bow before God in a much healthier picture of family and community relationships than Joseph's earlier dreams. Joseph then settles his family in Egypt, as an extension of his own privileged status in the land. His political and economic decisions are described in some detail – and the detail is worth pondering side by side with the story of Exodus in the key text Genesis 47.13–26.

To his mind, Joseph acts as a prudent, effective ruler who staves off famine and increases the power of Pharaoh, his master, by selling the grain he had commandeered in times of plenty, and taking people's farms and livelihoods, followed by their bondage, as payment. Yet what the story here suggests is that it is the combined energies of Joseph and Pharaoh that were the source of widespread slavery in Egypt. At a time of distress and famine, the rulers of Egypt used the famine for their own benefit. They did not simply look after the welfare of the people. Those who were already privileged – Pharaoh and his court, increased their wealth; those who had some privilege, the priests, were not exploited; those who were vulnerable and without access to power had what little they had – cattle, land and their own bodies – taken away from them. The men responsible for the common good exploited the people's desperation to expand their wealth and power. Furthermore, Joseph's actions not only breed injustice in the present, but set up a system that embeds injustice in the very fabric of the nation. Different castes of people are created and more strongly delineated through what he does. Taking away land and cattle meant that the people's existence became much more precarious, and prevented them from benefiting from their own work. Marx would say that Joseph effectively took control of 'the means of production'. By gaining control of most of the capital in the land, the wealthy grow wealthier, and pass on inherited wealth and privilege to their children, thereby reinforcing social divisions across generations. The picture is a dark one, and begs questions of how we assess business decisions within a framework of justice for all, rather than profit for the few.

It is easy to look back and think, this would never happen now! Yet a cursory glance at the events of the pandemic tells us that the human heart has not changed much. Some countries – the wealthy ones – had comprehensive pandemic plans in place, which were put in effect with varying degrees of success. Nations collaborated worldwide to develop a vaccine at breakneck speed, and wealthy, Western countries vaccinated their people faster than many could have imagined. Yet other entire countries are struggling to get hold of vaccines and, when they do, struggling to distribute them as they do not have the necessary infrastructure. Covid-19 is fast becoming a disease of the poor; those countries that have less access to medical care and sanitation are more vulnerable in the first place, less able to purchase vaccines, and less able to distribute them. Western countries, at the time of writing, have pledged to donate vaccines to others, but the numbers are small, and each country cares for its own first, as disputes about who should get vaccines being produced in various places have shown. The logic of Egypt, the logic of scarcity and efficiency, says that it makes good sense to look after yourself and 'your' people first. It is a logic that does not value all human lives equally, and difficult to counter in practice. Didn't Joseph have the right to care for his family first? Wasn't he right to maximize returns for his employer? After all, Pharaoh invested in systems to facilitate the retention and storage of grain in ways that kept Egypt from starving. Yet what might work at a micro level, only considering a subset of the population, quickly looks different at a macro level. Joseph had compassion for those he could see, his brothers and father, but none for the men and women who tilled the land, whom he did not see as clearly. The parameters established to judge his success within his sphere of influence – as Pharaoh's employee – do not take into account compassion, grace, generosity or the good of all humanity.

The story of Joseph forms a challenging backdrop for what comes next. Joseph stands in between Israel and Egypt, just as Moses will, but his contribution is to take Israel deeper into Egypt's imagination. The story complexifies our reading of Exodus. First, it undermines the clear Israel/Egypt distinction. Exodus may focus specifically on Israel and the additional ethnic-based pressures that they face, but the story of Joseph reminds us that the vast majority of Egyptians were treated badly too, were vulnerable and oppressed and in need of liberation. The logic of Egypt is the logic of rulers. Second, the story fits within a biblical pattern of drawing attention to the fragility of power and prosperity. Nations rise and fall, Israel goes in and out of favour. Third, it links back to the theme of the transgenerational impact of one's actions: Jacob's favouritism created Joseph's sense of superiority and the rift between siblings; Joseph's brothers' actions induced trauma, and Joseph being taken to Egypt, and there, shaped in ways far different from the covenant, Joseph's actions create conditions that make the enslavement of his people possible.

The story shows that Israel's imagination needed converting long before the events of Exodus, and that the conditions that shape Egypt are not unique: all human beings, even those that profess to follow God, are vulnerable. Lloyd Webber's musical is famous for its theme song, 'Any Dream Will Do'. But the actual story shows that not any dream will do. Some dreams are deeply damaging. Joseph's dreams of superiority are damaging, his brothers' dreams of revenge are damaging, and Joseph's vision for government is damaging. What Egypt and Israel both need, in Exodus, is a new dream, a new vision for who they may be.

Going back to the Joseph story does not justify in any way what happens to his descendants; but it does highlight the need for every person's imagination to be converted and reoriented in ways that are shaped by divine, rather than human principles.

The risks of a captive imagination

Joseph and Egypt illustrate the risks of a captive imagination; if the people go forward into the promised land, but take Egypt with them in their minds and social structures, what then? Scripture highlights the risks of an unconverted imagination again and again by calling Israel to remember Egypt, and do differently. Exodus, Leviticus and Deuteronomy all reinforce the need for Israel to remember that they once were slaves and aliens, so that they deal with slaves, aliens and one another differently.

In Deuteronomy 5.15, the memory of slavery reinforces the need to observe the Sabbath, so that the (unethical) work ethic of Egypt would not be reproduced; Deuteronomy 15.15 appeals to Israel's past to underlie laws about the compassionate treatment of slaves and servants, and 16.12, to justify right treatment of the most vulnerable social groups – the widow, the orphan and the stranger. In a similar vein, Deuteronomy 10.19 and Leviticus 19.34 remind Israel that they must treat the stranger well, because they themselves were strangers. It would be easy for a vulnerable, traumatized people, finding themselves suddenly powerful, with God on their side, to reproduce the structures of Egypt and simply reverse the poles of oppression, so that Hebrews were powerful and privileged, and others enslaved and mistreated. God's instructions, however, are crystal clear. Israel's liberation was not an end in and of itself. They were liberated for a purpose: to be a light to the nations by embodying a different, divine order. This new order would represent true freedom, a stepping away from the binary dynamics of self/other, Egyptian/Hebrew, citizen/stranger, poor/rich, master/slave, oppressor/victim, with compassion, equality and dignity defining social organization. To live justly may start with bringing down structures of oppressive power and lifting up the downtrodden, but it cannot stop there. To live justly is to seek new and restored structures of social belonging and interaction, which hold together justice and worship.

Exodus therefore stresses the communal, structural and political aspects of justice and sin. Establishing justice is core to the revelation of God in Exodus, through liberation and the formation of a new, converted community. This commitment is practical and all-encompassing. God does not just deal with private religious faith, but with structures and systems, and intervenes in history, to right wrongs and reorder broken relationships.

Being the people of God

Exodus calls the liberated people to truly become a 'people'. They are invited, at Sinai, to claim their identity as the redeemed people of God, freed from slavery, ready for something new. Before they leave Egypt, they had to self-identify as Hebrews, by spreading lamb blood over the lintels and doorposts of their houses. Interestingly, this command does not actually divide the residents of Egypt between ethnic Egyptians and ethnic Hebrews, or between different social classes. All who follow God's instructions will be saved, their firstborn spared. Belonging to the people of God is based primarily on obedience, trust and the need for liberation. Within the narrative of justice, there is room for mercy for those who choose to take it. This is another part of the story that is often less apparent, and less recounted.

As Israel moves into the desert, triumphalism makes way for the complex reality of forming a new community: ideals are wonderful, but the people are still people, frail, imperfect and traumatized. The pull of Egypt comes through powerfully in the story of the golden calf: while Moses is up on the mountain, speaking with God and receiving instructions to shape a just community, the people tire of waiting for a God they cannot easily see, hear or touch, and make an idol of gold. Very quickly, they go from worshipping the God who actually 'brought them out of Egypt' to worshipping an idol and claiming the manmade idol brought them out (Exodus 32.4). God's liberation is quickly reduced to what humans can claim for themselves. The unconverted imagination fails to see God at work, and seeks to claim a higher role for human beings than their nature and abilities warrant. A god made of gold is much less demanding, and dispenses with the need to change how they think and behave. The God of Exodus is not an easy God to worship.

Yet mercy is woven through the entire narrative. The episode of the golden calf brings judgement on the people for their choices, an accountability that recognizes their free will and the need to face the consequences of their actions; yet, at the same time, God shows himself committed to walking through these consequences together with his people. Failure is not the final word. As Moses had received the words of the Ten Commandments on the mountain, those laws had started with the statement of God's jealousy, and finished with a brief promise of love. In light of the people's actions, Moses receives another version of the law in Exodus 34, but this time the description of the character of God is rooted first in love and mercy, with a shorter statement of judgement that pales in contrast to the immensity of grace:

> The LORD, the LORD,
> a God merciful and gracious,
> slow to anger,
> and abounding in steadfast love and faithfulness,
> keeping steadfast love for the thousandth generation,
> forgiving iniquity and transgression and sin,
> yet by no means clearing the guilty,
> but visiting the iniquity of the parents
> upon the children
> and the children's children,
> to the third and the fourth generation.
> (Exodus 34.6–7)

As the people journey away from Egypt, their understanding of God is reshaped, away from judgement first (obvious to those watching the plagues), to mercy first. The story is crucial in understanding liberation and justice in God's eye, as Nathan Bills (2020, p. 252) puts it:

> [It] keeps Israel's incredible privilege (their election) in building for justice from becoming an arrogant swagger of possessing justice. The story is rigorously self-critical. It is a chastened Israel, enlivened by their liberation from evil both without and within, that now engages the good work of building for justice in a way reflecting God's character.

How we call for justice

The thread of mercy and compassion that runs through Exodus is a challenge to all who call for justice: how do we do so with all the passion we can muster, yet remain faithful to an imagination that refuses the easy categories of our surrounding cultures? How do we call for justice in prophetic ways, that is, both deeply rooted in our stories of faith and casting a vision for a different world?

Exodus is a prophetic book; its stories are not merely of past events, but meant to shape the present of its readers and offer a vision for a possible future. They give us a shape for recognizing injustice, hope in resisting it, even when we feel powerless, and guidance in how to shape the struggle. Prophets are usually passionate, they use every word and symbol at their disposal to shock others into hearing and seeing the oppressed, so that they can enter into the reality of those they had previously not seen. Prophetic voices are not reasoned voices, they are rooted in compassion and pain, in particular people, places and situations. The biblical prophets are often uncomfortable to read, and use images that we might find distasteful or even unhelpful. They have sharp edges.

Sometimes the model of biblical prophets is twisted out of shape when we try and call for justice, and forget the shape given by the biblical narrative: a shape rooted in ruthless honesty about our own limitations as human beings, our complete dependence on God for shaping our ability to recognize and do justice, and a profound anchoring in compassion that sees people – all people – as human beings, not caricatures or projections. The task of the prophet is to enable the people to see what is wrong, to enter into the suffering and call for redress, yet to do so in ways that bear the seeds of a different world; a world that does not reverse the poles of oppression and seek to annihilate the other, but a world that can imagine the wolf lying with the lamb, to use Isaiah's image. The prophets call for justice, but, together with their call, a warning and a lament often coincide, for they know what judgement means for the people. It is this joining together of passion for justice and awareness and compassion for the cost of justice that makes their call more than a strident condemnation. The late Supreme Court judge Ruth Baden Ginsburg, herself an ardent campaigner for justice, put it this way: 'Fight for the things you believe, but only in a way that makes people join you.'

Exodus is a story that is uncomfortable because it is radical – it proclaims that oppression is not inevitable, that freedom is possible, and that tyrants will be called to account. It is uncomfortable because it challenges all its characters to be transformed, regardless of their position in the story. And it is challenging, because it calls us to see the world with different lenses, and recognize the humanity of those whom we would rather not even see. Pharaoh is forced to see people he had wanted to suppress, and even annihilate. The Hebrews have a leader in Moses whose life and skills were made possible by the mercy of an Egyptian woman, Pharaoh's daughter, who disrupted the system from the inside. She not only defied her father, but took Moses in, paid his mother to nurse him – in contrast to slavery – and placed a despised Hebrew at the very centre of privilege. The story disrupts easy categorizations and prevents a new ethnocentric bias to develop, as former Chief Rabbi Jonathan Sacks (2010, p. 28) argues:

> Instead of Pharaoh's daughter, read 'Hitler's daughter', or 'Stalin's daughter' and we see what is at stake . . . That the Torah itself tells the story the way it does has enormous implications. It means that when it comes to people, we must never generalize, never stereotype. The Egyptians were not all evil: even from Pharaoh himself a heroine is born. Nothing could signal more powerfully that the Torah is not an ethnocentric text; that we must recognise virtue wherever we find it, even among our enemies; and the basic core of human values – humanity, compassion, courage – is truly universal. Holiness may not be; goodness is.

Questions for reflection

1 What do you think of Joseph's actions? Are there questions you would want to ask today's 'rulers' about how economic priorities and decisions are made?

2 Israel had to choose to put blood on their doors to identify as God's people; what identifies you, your family, your community, as 'God's people'?
3 Are there groups of people who are rendered one-dimensional in the way that social media and mainstream media speak of them? Why do you think that is? Are there ways for you to meet the people behind the caricatures?

A story from the United States

I've heard the cry of the modern-day prophets, 'Justice is what love looks like in public.' But I must begin with an admission I have always found it a struggle to live out along my activist journey. I'll begin as we Christians do, with a story.

My identity as an activist brought me to this moment facing off against Boston Police officers in front of a central bank building. Excited after a long march, my comrades and I yelled obscenities as only a crowd could conjure. I remember the moment quite clearly. I saw her. This woman's face wasn't as mean or as mocking as the rest of the police; she just seemed . . . concerned. I directed my ire towards her: 'Don't you have children? Do they know what you are doing here?' Then it hit me – maybe she does have children, maybe a partner, maybe brothers and sisters, for certain she has parents. She is a person with a whole life and a whole identity independent of what she is doing now. I saw her. Now, I could also see us; I could hear our words and see our faces: they were distorted, disfigured, so ugly. Something in me broke.

At this moment, I had to confront a question Howard Thurman articulates in his work *Disciplines of the Spirit*: 'Is what I am doing an expression of my fundamental intent toward any [person] when I am most myself?' Here my identity as an activist collided with my identity as a believer in the inherent dignity and worthiness of every human being and our indisputable connectedness – in short, my identity as a follower of Christ.

In the decade since this moment, I've been working through the tension between Love and Justice. This journey has led me to some wild experiences and diverse communities across the USA and around the globe. Thankfully, as with most of these large questions, I am not the first person to wrestle with this tension, much of the history of this inquiry is captured within our great religious traditions. I've been blessed to engage with scholars, activists, community leaders, the deeply invested and the sincerely disinterested, and my journey has led me to this conclusion:

A spirit of retaliation has come to dominate movements for justice that are arising in response to new and old divisions and evils across the globe. This spirit is not opposed to the division but in fact colludes with it. A successful confrontation with this division and evil requires the cultivation of a spirit of reconciliation, its true opposite. The cultivation of this spirit must become the primary work of religious communities in the twenty-first century.

I have been hesitant to fully articulate this conclusion. First, it isn't very original, and my millennial ego is telling me that 'if you're not saying something new, you're not really saying nothing at all'. But secondly, and much closer to the heart, I hesitate because I sense the ways that this conclusion alienates me from communities of justice-seekers and the disinherited, whom I love. I fear this will separate me from my communities as this conclusion and the action it demands will be perceived as giving shelter to those we have identified as enemies and placing unfair burdens on those whom we call victims.

I am fearful both because I don't want to be isolated from my communities but also because God's people have suffered long enough under leaders and ideologies that readily overlook them and are willing to trade away their humanity for symbolic concessions. I know the hurt and pain – I hear the cry of the disinherited. I am the disinherited. I know the heart and the sincerity of allies who yield to the pain in the collective body and rise up against oppression. I am an ally. I know and feel and yet I hear the whisper that says, 'Go deeper'. The call to seek and reclaim the common humanity of all of God's people trapped in systems and ideologies that distort us all into ugly things demands not a reaction but a response. The call of my saviour and the authentic response of my heart is to love. To somehow figure out how, in the midst of this apocalypse, to fight hard. Love as well as Justice.

After the police killing of George Floyd that set the world aflame in 2020 I had many friends from around the country and around the world reach out to me. Some to lament. Some to organize. Some just trying to understand. At times, I found it difficult to engage because the reality seemed so obvious and tragic to me; the same thing is always happening in this land plagued by demons groaning to be put to rest. I've committed myself to this struggle and expect much heartbreak but for many this pain was new.

During the Atlanta uprising I really began to question myself and my work. My commitment to reconciliation felt so hollow after watching police officers shoot Rayshard Brooks in the back, at a place I used to buy chicken nuggets in a neighbourhood where I used to live. I prayed and asked God where was my place in all of this? My prayer was answered the next morning, a mentor called and asked me if I would be willing to serve as a protest chaplain the next day.

On the ground, I could feel the hurt and the pain of that community. Standing in between protesters and police I recalled that moment years ago where I began to rethink my approach to activism. But this time it felt right to be there. I was there to bear witness. I looked into people's eyes as they watched buildings around them burn. I looked into the eyes of officers as they were confronted by the community they harmed. I heard and held many stories. I was there to declare with my presence that God did not forget these people.

From this place of non-judgement and (mostly) non-action something became clear. Reconciliation cannot begin without the development of some level of sensitiveness on the part of those who are unreconciled, they must first be able to see each other in order to break mimetic cycles of violence. In this present moment I fear it is not just that we choose not to see each other, but that we are losing the ability to do so.

Despite this assessment I can testify to great work being done in every corner of the world for the cause of Justice through loving action which makes possible reconciliation. I am filled with hope witnessing amazingly creative and loving responses to human tragedy. I am convinced that we already have everything we need to transform conflict, bridge divides and heal our collective wounds. The problem is merely one of exposure. We need the work being done on the margins to be called into the center of our daily experience and our religious institutions must become spaces where this work is made visible. While it seems dark we just need more folks pointing in the direction of the light. It is there I promise. I've seen it!
(Demarius J. Walker)

Prayer

One of the most beautiful prayers for justice in Scripture is Mary's Magnificat, in Luke 1.46–55:

My soul magnifies the Lord,
    and my spirit rejoices in God my Saviour,
for he has looked with favour on the lowliness of his servant.
    Surely, from now on all generations will call me blessed;
for the Mighty One has done great things for me,
    and holy is his name.
His mercy is for those who fear him
    from generation to generation.
He has shown strength with his arm;
    he has scattered the proud in the thoughts of their hearts.
He has brought down the powerful from their thrones,
    and lifted up the lowly;
he has filled the hungry with good things,
    and sent the rich away empty.

He has helped his servant Israel,
   in remembrance of his mercy,
according to the promise he made to our ancestors,
   to Abraham and to his descendants for ever.

3

Building communities of justice

Legal systems and community justice

One of the best known verses about justice in the Bible is the often quoted Micah 6.8: 'He has told you, O mortal, what is good; and what does the LORD require of you but to do justice, and to love mercy, and to walk humbly with your God?' It's a great verse, which captures the relationship between justice and compassion/ mercy, and the link with worship. However, it is often so divorced from its context that it is hard to know exactly what it means. How do we stop the word 'justice' from becoming an empty cipher for whatever our background culture and ideology tells us we should desire? The word in Scripture is invested with meaning by being tied to a story, a people, a time and place. When the verse is used in Christian worship, we often hear an individual appeal to examine ourselves and be good people, to think about our use of money, and how we treat others day to day. Micah, however, is addressing a community; of course individuals have a role to play and need to examine themselves, but it is the people *as a whole* that have to do justice and love mercy. How differently do we hear these words if we hear them in relation to the different communities we belong to: families, churches, workplaces, towns, nations, the entire world? The prophet's appeal places people in relationship to one another, with a presumption of mutual accountability and responsibility. It is individuals-in-community who are addressed, and more than one-to-one human relationships. Concern for the entire work-ings of community, institutions and culture, puts 'justice' in the prophets in deep continuity with everything that has come before, including the foundational events of Exodus.

Exodus had marked not just the end of slavery for the people of Israel, but the beginning of something new, an invitation to live as the people of God, shaped by God's character. We cannot understand Exodus fully unless we understand what the newly free people are called to, and we cannot understand what they are called to unless we understand what they are freed from. Justice in response to oppression and justice in creating a non-oppressive community are two sides of the same coin. The most salient aspect of the new life they are invited into is that it is life *together*. Together with God, and together as a people. In the texts that set out principles, laws and vision for how they might live, there is a constant interplay between people, God and land, with just relationships at the very centre. People, God and land always come with a context, embedded in history, geography and culture, so the story is shaped and, at times, limited by its specificity: the laws that are given make sense for the Ancient Near East and draw on shared culture with other ancient people; the vision is for an agrarian, non-industrial society organized around extended households; the people meant to catch the vision are not perfect, and the laws and guidance they are given do not pretend that they can be. The story explores the art of the possible, and how the possible interacts with the ideal. This pragmatic, realistic streak is one, paradoxically, that sustains hope: the people often fail and get it wrong, but God still walks with them. Israel's struggle to live justly reflects our own ambivalence about justice – whether we want it, or even want to want it – and proclaims that our stumblings towards justice are never the final word. The concessions to culture and what is possible are a mark of patience and grace on God's part, and resonate with the picture of a God who chooses to live with his people, to enter into their pain, rather than give orders from on high.

Because the people are called as a people, they have to learn to organize themselves in new ways, put in place systems, institutions and practices that will enable justice in every way – in shaping the community, and in responding to inevitable evil within and without.

Justice is relationship

The law chapters of the Old Testament are rarely anyone's favourites. From Exodus to Leviticus to Deuteronomy, pages and pages record different directives for the people to organize themselves, to respond to accidents, natural phenomena and evil, directions on what to eat, on familial relationships, extensive prescriptions regarding worship, and much more. Many of these texts seem alien and removed. How can they speak today, given our different preoccupations, values and understanding of what it means to be human? There is no easy answer; the Bible cannot be dissected, mined for principles we can abstract from stories and people and simply reapply today. What we can do, however, is read it in openness to how God was working with his people then, and lay the stories alongside ours, and ask, does reading this story challenge the way I tell mine or ours? Does my/our story prompt questions about the text that we need to wrestle with in prayer?

The idea that justice is communal and relational is obviously not only to be found in Scripture. Justice is by definition interpersonal, concerned with how human beings relate or fail to relate, and justice is needed because human beings cannot live independently. Because they need one another to survive, they also need systems to regulate their lives and enable all members to play their part. Here, however, is where consensus ends. Not every society agrees that everyone has a part to play, or gifts to give; nor do they agree on what the best systems may be to ensure that the community as a whole thrives. Theories of justice extend from the strongly libertarian, who would want a minimal state, with a high degree of personal freedom and rights, to those who advocate for a strong, centralized state to curb the human tendency to selfishness and self-preservation. Different social justice campaigners have different ideas of what 'good' looks like. Increasingly multicultural societies will inevitably hold different ideas of justice, and struggle to develop a vision that is not reduced to the lowest common denominator, or oppressively asserting one vision over all others.

Much against my better judgement, I once got into a heated discussion about refugees on social media. Social media is not really the best place to discuss complex issues in grown-up ways. But the exchange was illuminating, and gave me much food for thought. The discussion thread followed a news report of a boat full of desperate people sinking in the Mediterranean – a frequent occurrence still, as refugees desperate to find safety and a better life are promised safe passage in thoroughly unsafe conditions. I made a simple point about the fact that all of us belong to the human race, that we are interconnected, and, by virtue of our common humanity, have responsibilities towards one another, as people and as nations. One of the responses was,

> Well, I agree, but you can't impose that philosophy on every-one. I might think that I have a duty to help others, but that's my choice, and you can't say that all human beings have duties to help one another. That's just one opinion.

Therein lies the problem in talking of justice: if there is no wider frame of reference, no sense that there are standards somehow external to ourselves, it is very difficult to agree on what justice looks like, and without agreement, it is difficult to put in place systems and institutions that reflect just values. A common vision for justice, or enough of a common vision, is necessary to enable individuals to become a community, rather than a collection of separate entities sometimes working together if it benefits them or fits their own standards. The comment on social media was typical of the privatization of ethics that we saw at work in the very first story of human beings in Scripture: wanting to decide what is good and bad for ourselves, without reference to God, or anyone else.

As a child, growing up in Republican France, the values of the Republic were drilled into us: liberty, equality, fraternity. We explored those in 'civic education' lessons. I do not remember much about those, apart from the mantra repeated over and over again, that my freedom always stops where yours begins, and that I only have freedom because you limit your own in order to grant me freedom. It is not a bad thing to have remembered. The foundational principle we were taught was that human beings are interdependent, that 'freedom' is necessarily relational and involves a trade-off between rights and responsibilities. Freedom is a gift that we give one another. Liberty is only possible with equality and fraternity: it needs to acknowledge the fundamental dignity of other human beings, and individualism needs to be tempered by solidarity. Equality inescapably involves freedom, because a lack of freedom denies the dignity of the other person, and solidarity inherently seeks equality as an expression of care for the other. We could debate the rights and wrongs of that vision (the French do, a lot!), but what it does is create a context within which there are enough shared principles to undergird a vision of justice and the common good, even when we disagree on how to get there.

The principles that shaped the French vision were partly secular (it is obvious in the language), yet still deeply shaped by France's long history as a Christian country, even as France often tries to deny its roots. The imagination of the Christian Scriptures, when it comes to justice, are rooted in the Old Testament, where the key concepts are not autonomy and rights, but interdependence and responsibilities. Human beings are not simply 'an aggregate of individuals pursuing private interests, coming together temporarily and contractually, leaving the state to resolve their conflicts on value-neutral grounds . . . free to act as [they] please so long as [they] do not harm others', as often seems the case today (Sacks, 1995, p. 11). Rather, human beings have a claim on one another: they have a moral obligation to look out for the welfare of the other as made in the image of God. It is these mutual obligations that create 'rights', but these rights are preceded by responsibilities. In this context,

> justice creates a sphere of mutual obligations that extends through the whole community, rulers no less than subjects, rich and powerful no less than weak and poor, one culture no less than the other. Justice forms the basis for cohesion and solidarity.
> (Volf, 1996, p. 196)

Questions for reflection

1 If France's vision of justice is based on 'liberty, equality, fraternity', what three words would sum up your own vision? Your community's? Your country's?

2 Do you think there are universal rules for justice, or obligations, that all human beings are under? If not, why not? If yes, what might those be?

3 How can the Old Testament framework of responsibilities before rights help us seek justice?

The laws of the Old Testament

Big picture, small picture

When someone mentions justice, people often think of two things. One is, what's fair or unfair, how everyone gets their due, how a society lives in equitable ways ('distributive' justice). The other is the justice system and its laws. The two are closely related, and come to prominence in different situations. The first is largely what we have been looking at so far: how a society is organized to ensure fair access to freedom, goods, opportunities, influence and a fair distribution of duties and responsibilities. Justice is often reduced to questions of economics and distribution of wealth, maybe because it is the easier problem to solve and avoids deeper questions around the value of every human being, and the claims that we may have on one another. The biblical concept of justice is much wider, rooted in the character of God and the abundance of creation. Justice is not primarily about deserts, but about compassion, grace, generosity and community obligations. In a world dominated by an economy of scarcity, however, societies wrestle with the unequal organization of goods and power, and those with power and wealth usually seek to keep it, whether by force or careful political and economic lobbying. The tension is as present in the stories of Scripture as it is on the pages of newspapers today.

The book of Job tells the story of a man who was immensely wealthy and very pious, at a time when at least a segment of the population assumed that wealth equalled blessing – that is, wealth, health, family, status and power were deserved and based on merit or righteousness. Job, however, finds that the balance of his universe crumbles; he unexpectedly loses everything – family, wealth, health and, with them, status and power. Friends come to comfort him, and do what people often do: they try to find a rational explanation for Job's reversal of fortunes. Their ideas are familiar today too: 'Job, it must be your fault! You must have done something wrong, it must be a punishment. Maybe God wants to teach you something.' In other words – Job, you deserve it. To acknowledge that misfortune and pain can happen to anyone, that life simply is not fair, is too threatening for Job's comfortable friends. It would make the precariousness of their lives too real, and therefore they comfort themselves – rather than Job – with an illusion of order that preserves their own power and status, and enables them to shrug off the obligation to care for their friend, as of equal standing, righteousness and ability. Fortunately, the story does not end there, as God appears, and, in the end, rebukes the friends for their false comforts, and commends Job for speaking rightly:

> After the LORD had spoken these words to Job, the LORD said to Eliphaz the Temanite: 'My wrath is kindled against you and against your two friends; for you have not spoken of me what is right, as my servant Job has. Now therefore take seven bulls and seven rams, and go to my servant Job, and offer up for yourselves a burnt-offering; and my servant Job shall pray for you, for I will accept his prayer not to deal with you according to your folly; for you have not spoken of me what is right, as my servant Job has done.'
> (Job 42.7–8)

What did Job do? He ranted and raved and raged against life and against God; he recognized the utter injustice and meaninglessness of his circumstances, and pleaded for compassion. The book of Job undermines the idea that poverty, ill health and general misfortune are in humanity's control, or that the poor deserve to be poor and the rich, rich. Human beings do have agency, but, ultimately, no overall control, and no right to assume that another person is lesser than them because of their external circumstances. Life sometimes gets in the way of even the most hard-working, moral, well-intentioned people, and the way forward is not philosophy, but compassion and solidarity. Job's misfortunes put a claim to compassion on those who surround him.

This wider framework is essential before the second aspect of justice, often called retributive or remedial justice, is put in place. The nature of the remedy or retribution depends on how the problem was defined in the first place. It is no accident that Israel had to learn the practice of justice through manna and Sabbath in the desert, before they even begin to put in place a complex system of governance and law in the promised land. The reality of fallen humanity dictates that wonderful ideas about justice need concrete frameworks for implementation, and the possibility of redress when things go wrong. The people are taught about divine justice, but this justice needs embodying through people and systems.

What are laws for?

My father was a lawyer. He became a lawyer out of an idealist vision of what the world could be like. He had grown up in poor surroundings, his parents tenant farmers with many children. He was put to work at 14 to help support the rest of the family at a time when small farms became largely unviable. By 20, he decided to try for more and resumed his education. By the time I was at school, we were having legal discussions at the dinner table, when he told us about process and technicalities. I struggled to see the connection between his early youthful passion for equality and justice, and the reality of a legal system within which process at times mattered more than truth. It took me a long time to understand. Laws do not create justice, they merely make it possible. Laws point to a deeper vision of what life could be, but they do not inherently have the power to create that vision. They simply give a framework within which it is possible to pursue justice and enable human flourishing. In the same way that getting a driving licence does not make me a brilliant driver, the laws of a country do not make it a just, wonderful place. They establish a minimum standard within which it is possible for the vision to take root. The level of this 'minimum' varies hugely, and the variations are rooted into the deeper vision that animates them. There is a dynamic relationship between vision and law. If the vision does not see every person as equal, laws will be made that do not give those who are 'less equal' the same degree of protection or access to goods as others, or at least fail to be applied in equal ways. Neither the vision nor the laws are static; they evolve in history, with culture, knowledge and world events.

Students of the Old Testament often puzzle about its laws, finding them repulsive in today's context. Leaving aside the question of interpretation and whether they understand the text, this instinctive reaction reveals how understandings of the right relationships between human beings and the right order of the world have changed. What made sense in the Middle Eastern Bronze Age unsurprisingly makes less sense in the twenty-first century. Yet instead of immediately taking a stance of judgement and cultural superiority, we might open ourselves to a dialogue between the world of the text and the world of today. What do our instinctive reactions tell us? If we are shocked by what we see as injustice, what has changed in our view of humanity to take us to this point? If the laws in the text are culturally relevant and reflect accommodation to time and place, how do our laws do the same, and reflect our own limitations? What would the people of the text baulk at in our legal systems and visions of the world? Can we bring these two worlds before God, and ask the Spirit to help us discern where God is at work in both, and what might need adapting, changing or reconsidering? I often wonder what the people of the ancient world, with their constant focus on interdependence with the land and natural environment, would think of our treatment of the earth today, and the laws and systems we have created that make it so difficult to deal with climate change. Or, reflecting on the Covid-19 pandemic and its enormous toll on older generations, particularly in nursing homes in the West, what would the people of Scripture, in a culture that treasured and respected age and wisdom, have to say about how we speak of old age, value our elders, and position them within our societies?

To understand the legal texts, and how they may help us think about justice, we need first to identify how different they are from the way we might think about law today. First, the law codes of Israel are similar to others from the Ancient Near East in their general philosophy, the questions they pose, and the type of answer they give. These laws are therefore incarnated into a time and culture, not disembodied or timeless. The similarities highlight the fact that justice can be found elsewhere, and is not the sole possession of Israel. All human beings, made in the image of God, have a capacity to think justly and recognize ways of being consonant with God's image. Whether in Israel or surrounding countries, there is no evidence that law codes (sets of material as we find for instance in Exodus 21.1—23.33) were used to settle disputes. There is plenty of evidence of court cases and judicial proceedings, but not that they used law codes, which suggests that these laws were not intended to be used in the way we would today.

What is striking, however, particularly in Scripture, is the number of laws undergirded by a motive (something that does not happen here in the West when we write down our laws):

You shall not wrong or oppress a resident alien, for you were aliens in the land of Egypt.
(Exodus 22.21)

If you take your neighbour's cloak in pawn, you shall restore it before the sun goes down; for it may be your neighbour's only clothing to use as cover; in what else shall that person sleep? And if your neighbour cries out to me, I will listen, for I am compassionate.
(Exodus 22.26–27)

You shall not oppress a resident alien; you know the heart of an alien, for you were aliens in the land of Egypt.
(Exodus 23.9)

For six days you shall do your work, but on the seventh day you shall rest, so that your ox and your donkey may have relief, and your home-born slave and the resident alien may be refreshed.
(Exodus 23.12)

About 5 per cent of surrounding nations' laws had these explanations. In Scripture, it is nearly half (Evans, 2015, p. 7). These explanations point to the purpose of the laws: to develop moral

thinking and community values, which will then guide the administration of justice. They are meant to develop Israel's imagination
and enable every person to appropriate the spirit of the law, not
because it is imposed from on high, but because they understand its rightness and purpose. Despite similarities to other law
codes, the biblical texts contain striking differences, which show
how they are an encouragement to enlarge the imagination and
push the boundaries of the surrounding culture, without being
divorced from their specific place and time. Laws have to make
sense for people to follow them. They can push the boundaries to
a certain degree, but they need to remain interconnected with the
way people think, feel and organize life for them to have currency.
These laws demonstrate, once again, the art of the possible, and
how vision meets practice. The laws of Israel were therefore not
just a legal repository, but a way to remember stories and values;
laws today often have their origins in specific contexts – so, for
instance, the tightening of gun ownership in the UK after the
Dunblane massacre, where a gunman shot 16 pupils and a teacher
in a primary school; or, Megan's Law in the United States, enacted
after the murder of a young girl by a sex offender. Yet today we
rarely inscribe the story into the text of the law, so that laws become
disembodied, as if they were universal and eternal rather than
responsive to time and place, and, as culture moves on, the reason
for the law becomes lost.

In many ancient cultures, punishment and justice varied with
status. It was not simply that the rich could hire better lawyers or
expert witnesses, but people were, quite literally, not equal before
the law. In biblical law, however, all citizens are, in principle, equal,
and bribery or partiality are severely condemned. While today
we find the punishments prescribed for various offences unpalat-
able (rightly so!), they were often much less severe than in other
nations: property crime was never punished with mutilation,
beating or death, and there are fewer calls for capital punishment.
The value of human life far surpasses that of property. The loss
and impairment of human life is considered with great care, and
slaves are not dealt with as purely economic property. Specific laws

seek to protect slaves, and if a master kills a slave, his life is forfeit, which implies they are equal in value. Multiple laws seek to protect the poor and curb the growth of wealth, and set an active require- ment to share wealth (Exodus 23.10–11). Concern for the alien is unique to Israel, rooted in Israel's experience in Egypt. Commands concerning care for aliens occur more frequently than commands about the Sabbath, circumcision, theft, falsehood or loving God.

How the laws are organized also sheds light on the vision under- neath: prescriptions are bookended with material about worship, and love of God, so that love and God and love of neighbour are inextricably linked. The very first laws given that are not about worship are laws about how to treat slaves and servants, and Israel's own experience is referred to repeatedly. Their experience of vul- nerability and oppression is also used countless times to undergird care for the vulnerable, with a warning that if the vulnerable are oppressed, they will cry out to God, and God will answer – just as God did in Exodus 2. The people are asked to identify with the vulnerable as a core aspect of their identity. It is not merely a call to compassion from outside, but to adopt a very specific posture in life, characterized by justice, rooted in the God who delivered the people from Egypt.

Here is the account of someone (name and details changed, and swearing removed) who was a probation officer for many years, telling of their frustration with the justice system. I interviewed them, and this is their story.

I became a probation officer many years ago, because I believed people could change. I wanted to make a difference and to help people, both offenders and victims. I listened to more stories than I can remember. Twenty years' worth of stories, sad and angry stories, from people lost in life, from people who were hurt, angry and bitter, some just sad, some evil. I also spent time in the victim contact unit, listening to the horrendous impact of violent and sexual crime on victims. My entire career was about making things change, so there would be less victims, so we would protect people, and help some of the most disadvantaged people in this country turn their lives around. Twenty years, and suddenly, I had a bad couple of months, and just lost it. You know when you get this sudden realization, what on earth am I doing this for? This is pointless. Meaningless. I just can't do it any more. I suppose it built up gradually and I didn't really notice – the frustration that I was allowed less and less time with clients, that rehabilitation was increasingly seen as a soft option. (Only those who haven't gone through it could say that. To get people to face the absolute worse of themselves and what they have done, and change, that isn't soft. It's flipping hard work. And it's the only way to protect the public, unless you keep more and more people in prison and throw away the key, and that costs a bomb.) But what got me in the end was the system, the courts, the stuff we call 'justice'. I had a series of cases in one month, and I had to write pre-sentence reports on all of them. [Pre-sentence reports assess the roots of offending behaviour, risk factors and protective factors, what can be done to help reduce offending, and recommendations on appropriate sentencing.] I got the court papers, with the witness statements, the police documents, and what the judge thought the right sentence might be. In one week I got four court referrals. One, two blokes had a bar fight. One of them got injured (not really badly). The judge said he wanted to impose a custodial sentence. The next one, another bloke, had committed 'theft from employer'. Embezzled £15,000. He had offered to repay, was happy to pay large amounts of compensation, to do community service, have a tag for a curfew. The judge wanted a custodial sentence. Both those did get sent to prison. In the same week, I had another referral. Two young men had abused the little sister of one of them, age 12 – abused her repeatedly over two years. She got pregnant and had an abortion. The judge wanted me to comment on community sentences because he didn't think it was serious enough for prison. I also had a domestic violence case. Some guy beat his partner to pulp, left her unconscious. Not the first time. She fled to a refuge with her daughter, and he tracked them down and threatened to kill the child in front of a refuge worker. He was put in a bail hostel pending sentence. The judge asked me to comment on a community sentence. I said no, he is too dangerous, and the judge said, he is well behaved in the hostel, there's no evidence he is dangerous. I quit. What's the point? What is the point? Money from an employer is worth more than a child. A bar fight between two drunks is more important than a vulnerable young mum and her daughter. It's madness. I know that the judge will say there are reasons, circumstances, that you need to look at the whole picture. That there were different judges for each case so you can't compare. But it still says something, doesn't it? About our values and our laws and what we care about. So I quit. Now I work with refugees, in a charity, listening to their stories and helping them to navigate the system. And I volunteer as a mentor for young offenders. All I ever wanted was to make a difference.

An eye for an eye leaves the whole world blind (Gandhi)

Israel did not simply have law codes to guide behaviour, they established, early on, a judicial system:

> You shall appoint judges and officials throughout your tribes, in all your towns that the LORD your God is giving you, and they shall render just decisions for the people. You must not distort justice; you must not show partiality; and you must not accept bribes, for a bribe blinds the eyes of the wise and subverts the cause of those who are in the right. Justice, and only justice, you shall pursue, so that you may live and occupy the land that the LORD your God is giving you.
> (Deuteronomy 16.18–20)

The establishment of this system is linked to welfare in the land, and the pursuit of justice more widely. Neutrality and impartiality are set as golden standards, not that they should block out human feelings and compassion, but in the sense that justice is administered from without a situation, with a strict prohibition against judges being swayed by personal gain, and against pure revenge. Devolving the resolution of disputes and harm to a judicial system proclaims that justice is not merely about individuals, but a matter for the community as a whole. Dealing with injustice publicly sets expectations and boundaries for the community that make it safe. When an offence is committed, the community as a whole is involved and needs to respond in order to nurture its common life.

In particular, the system is there to prevent both the unchecked exploitation of the vulnerable and an escalation of violence through ever-increasing cycles of revenge. The limitation of revenge is highlighted time and again in the Old Testament. The desire for vengeance is a common human response to deep hurt. In itself, it highlights the seriousness of sin, and the depth of damage caused by interpersonal violations and violence. What human beings do with these feelings of hurt, anger and desire for retaliation, however, matters greatly to the flourishing of a society.

Old Testament laws are seldom remembered or quoted, save one: 'an eye for an eye, a tooth for a tooth', the *lex talionis* (Exodus 21.24; Deuteronomy 19.21). What are we to make of this? Is this not vengeful? Imagine a nation without laws – does revenge tend to set limits? Revenge often takes far more than one eye for one eye, and blood feuds were common. As one person is hurt and strikes back, families and friends get involved and the conflict widens and escalates (see, for instance, the story of Dinah and Schechem in Genesis 34, where all the men in one city are killed in response to the horrendous crime of one of them). The *lex talionis* is not a requirement, but rather a limitation (Lynch, 2020, p. 128), which defines the absolute limit of what can be done, while still acknowledging harm. It sets an underlying principle about proportionality in justice. In contrast, vengeance is consistently frowned upon, and said to be the prerogative of God only.

The Old Testament clearly distinguishes between different types of offences and the penalties appropriate to each. Care is taken to distinguish between intentional and accidental harm. Restitution is a consistent feature. Property is of less value than human life, and the integrity of the body and the impact of violations of bodies and personhood are particularly significant and heinous. Not all harm is the same, and not all sins are equal. It was fashionable in a church I attended to hear, 'We are all sinners; it doesn't matter what your sin is, sin is sin, we are all the same before God.' At one level, this is true – no human being can ever take the high ground and claim they have never hurt anyone or done anything wrong. But that is very different from claiming that all sin is equal. The impact of different sins is very clearly differentiated in Scripture, not to introduce a hierarchy between offenders, but to attend to the depth of harm caused. It is the impact on victims that enables differentiation in legal terms. Hence, one of the functions of the judicial system is to bear witness to trauma and pain, and acknowledge the reality of the lived experience of victims. This differentiation is about honouring each person, their dignity, and the image of God within them.

Laws and judicial systems are far from perfect; they are embedded in a society and its values. But their presence is a testimony to that community's struggle to embody justice, as Barack Obama (1995, p. 437) beautifully puts it:

The study of law can be disappointing at times, a matter of applying narrow rules and arcane procedure to an uncooperative reality; a sort of glorified accounting that serves to regulate the affairs of those who have power – and that all too often seeks to explain, to those who do not, the ultimate wisdom and justness of their condition.

But that's not all the law is. The law is also memory; the law also records a long-running conversation, a nation arguing with its conscience.

Questions for reflection

1 Israel's laws are linked to their stories and vision; what kind of story do the laws of your country tell?
2 Are there any laws in the Old Testament you find difficult? Why are they challenging today? Would any of our laws or practices today be challenging to ancient Israelites?
3 How can you distinguish between justice and revenge?

The marks of a just community

The Jubilee laws
Key text: Leviticus 25.1–28

The Jubilee laws of Leviticus came to some notoriety with the Jubilee 2000 campaign, which focused on putting pressure on wealthy countries to cancel the debts of poorer countries. Those countries had already more than repaid the initial debt and were simply paying interest that kept accruing over the years. This was crippling their economies, whereas wealthy countries could afford to cancel these debts with minimal impact. The campaign name was taken directly from Leviticus. Historically, there is no evidence that these laws were ever put into practice, presumably because they were too radical. The Jubilee laws are not retributive or remedial but constructive laws, aimed to shape a just and fair society, and the imagination of its people. The Jubilee 2000 campaign extracted the principle of cancellation of debts after a certain number of years, but Leviticus gives a much more fulsome picture.

First, the land belongs to God. Resources are not freely at the disposal of human beings, they are given in trust to be managed justly, and the Jubilee laws ensure that they can be passed on justly to the next generation. Humans are dependent on the land for their very survival. It may be less obvious in urban cultures and industrialized nations, but they too depend on the land and its resources. To be just, a society has to maintain a just distribution of land and resources that enables all to survive. In Leviticus, any land sold reverts to its original inhabitants after a certain number of years, which makes senses in a family/household-based setting where the land had been parcelled out evenly between different tribes. Whatever is needed for survival cannot be removed permanently from other human beings. Economic logic may justify taking property or land away, but economics are never given the final word. Care for the vulnerable matters more, regardless of the reason why something was sold or pawned in the first place.

Grace and compassion are the bedrock of the social organization imagined here.

Second, the Jubilee laws actively mitigate against the accumulation of wealth and its attendant inherited privilege. No matter how hard someone has worked, they are not entitled to more than their fair share. And if someone loses their fair share, through no fault of their own (illness, natural disaster, war) or their own mismanagement, or a combination of both, this is not allowed to keep affecting generation after generation. The Jubilee laws aim to break down transgenerational cycles of power and powerlessness, privilege and disadvantage, by resetting the clock on a regular basis. Of course, some might say, 'But it's not fair! If I work hard, and save, and live well, why shouldn't my children inherit the fruit of my good life?' The problem with this is that it only makes sense at the micro level of one family, and does not consider the welfare of the whole nation. Limiting the possibility of passing on excessive wealth means there is less incentive to over-accumulate it in the first place, and greater incentive to live within the framework of the Sabbath. This law puts in place a practical system to ensure that the sins of fathers do not affect more than a few generations, whereas principles of right living, within the Sabbath economy, can keep being passed on to the thousandth generation. What might be 'appropriate provision' is, of course, somewhat complex to determine. The Jubilee laws do not prevent caring for the next generation; what they protect is the land, that is, the very possibility that the next generation might be able to care for themselves well. They prevent any one person or family from hoarding too high a share of resources that belong rightly with others. In addition, every generation has to work for itself, taking responsibility and contributing equally.

Finally, the laws of Jubilee posit the rights of the land and of its animals. Not only is the land God's land, but it has rights of its own and cannot simply be exploited by human beings. Even the land is entitled to its Sabbath rest – another antidote to the tyranny of productivity, and, for contemporary readers, an uncomfortable principle in the light of the current environmental crisis.

Why spend time thinking through laws that were never enforced – and probably unenforceable in the first place? Because they set that broad sense of how to be just, how to be human, how to live well. They provide context for all the other laws: so, for instance, when a law prescribes tithing, it is meant within a context in which all have, broadly speaking, adequate and fair incomes; hence the poor are not asked to give out of their necessary while the rich give out of their superfluous. The whole system works together. This then points us to a pressure point when we talk about justice: what is 'just' at a micro level often blinds us to the bigger picture. It is almost impossible for small transactions to be just unless the bigger picture is just too. In other words, retributive justice in specific cases is rarely just unless there is distributive justice at a wider level. What would this look like today?

Take some of the arguments around vaccine inequality during the pandemic. At a world level, there has been gross inequality in the ability of countries to purchase and distribute vaccine supplies, so that injustice is flagrant and deeply disturbing. Yet the many arguments that make the situation possible are made as micro-level arguments: the responsibility of leaders to care for their own countries; the rights of countries that invested the most to have privileged access; and laws around intellectual property and eco-nomics. Pharmaceutical companies did an extraordinary job of collaboration and research to discover a vaccine so quickly. But research is prohibitively expensive, especially when done at such speed. To balance the books, pharmaceutical companies have to charge effective prices for the vaccines, which in turn prevents poorer countries from acquiring sufficient quantities, and guard the formula for the vaccine, which prevents others from manufac-turing it at cheaper prices locally. The argument makes sense and seems 'fair' at the level of the company; the problem is that the overall, international system is unjust, privileges richer countries, and turns health into a marketable commodity. The conundrum can only be solved at the macro level; the G7 meeting pledged vaccines for Global South countries, but the numbers were far fewer than needed. The much more difficult work involves these leaders putting in place agreements to change how pandemics are responded to internationally. If they do strike an agreement however, some will deem it unfair to those who invested in the first place, just as those who worked hard and increased wealth but have to give it up under Jubilee laws may complain of unfairness. The problem of macro justice is that it relies on a shared vision for justice, for economics, for flourishing, for what it is to be human, for ethics, and the more people are involved, the more different cultures and contexts, the harder it is to coalesce around this vision.

A community centred on God

Given the difficulty of holding a common vision, it is unsurprising that the Jubilee laws and the wider legal material in Scripture imagines a just society as centred on God. God commands, 'be holy, for I am holy' (Leviticus 11.44–45; 19.2; 20.7). Holiness and justice are interlinked; the people are commanded to imitate God, so that the image of God can shine brightly in and through them. Because God is just, the people are called to be just. It is looking up to God, and reflecting his nature, that gives Israel the necessary cohesion to pursue a vision of justice together.

The laws are therefore part of the framework of covenant, based on God's initial compassion and grace. The covenantal framework makes it quite a different system from contemporary understandings such as either a horizontal social contract between the different members of a society, who trade a bit of their freedom to gain security through the rule of law, or the purely vertical individual–divine contract imagined in individualistic and libertarian contexts. Rather, it is a rich interweaving of mutual human obligations with a shared faith and relationship with God. It may be helpful to take a moment to ponder how this may transfer to our approach to justice in a church context: how do we understand our mutual responsibilities, and how they are woven into the fabric of how God builds the Church?

It is this covenantal framework that enables justice and mercy to be held together as natural partners, as they work jointly to deliver the oppressed and the marginalized, to challenge selfishness, injustice and exploitation and enable a realistic framework for peaceful communities that prize human dignity, peace and justice. The joining of the two prevents the justice framework from becoming legalistic and ruthless in its dealings with frail and fallen human beings. It is easy for the pursuit of equality and justice to expect more of other people, and of institutions, than we are able to achieve ourselves in most areas of life. Scripture is brutally honest about human nature: full of ambiguity and complexity, striving for justice in one area, yet blind in another, torn between good and bad, between selfishness and care for others.

This portrayal of human beings stands in stark contrast to many contemporary theories of justice, which rarely see human nature as inherently problematic, and either assume humanity to be altruistic or basically selfish (Forrester, 2001, p. 52). To forget these complexities inevitably leads to skewed and imperfect solutions: see, for instance, the way in which Marxism rests on a belief that it is possible for human beings to construct a community of justice and equality. History suggests that the approach was deeply flawed, as power struggles, selfishness and thirst for wealth and status undermined every practical attempt. In a completely different way, contemporary society often stresses therapeutic, person-centred approaches, that seek to understand the self, which is good, but avoid talk of guilt and sin; the risk there is to bypass the immense harm that sin does to other human beings and the wider world, so that the individual is absolved of responsibility and seen as entirely conditioned by their environment, with little free will. The Bible, in contrast, uses the categories of sin, guilt, judgement, grace and forgiveness to speak of justice. Such a view of human nature inevitably drives us deeper into the embrace of justice and mercy, and the need for provisionality, compassion and humility in any human verdict on another. It ensures that, by being confronted with our own sinfulness on the one hand, and the holiness of God on the other, seeking justice remains a vocation, rather than a crusade against neighbours (Brueggemann, 1982, p. 37).

To hold together justice and mercy recognizes that the past cannot be changed: retribution and reparation do not give redress for the past, and often risk creating new injustices in the present – as the ripple effect of any actions have unforeseen consequences and touch a wide circle of people; to find true justice is an ideal. In the world as it is, what is needed is for justice to be good enough, and therefore it needs a measure of grace and the acceptance of imperfections and that justice cannot change the past. What it can do is give a new shape to the future by reimagining how we can live together.

A shared responsibility

Whose responsibility is it to ensure justice, and work towards it? The Bible answers, quite clearly, everyone's. Every member of a community contributes to patterns of justice and injustice, has a responsibility to choose leaders wisely, to speak truth and confront evil. Justice is not the sole responsibility of leaders, or judicial functionaries, even though they have enhanced responsibilities. In the ancient world, kings had ultimate responsibility for justice; but at Sinai the people are given no human king. Instead, they are all invited to step into the splendour and responsibility of kingship:

> Now therefore, if you obey my voice and keep my covenant, you shall be my treasured possession out of all the peoples. Indeed, the whole earth is mine, but you shall be for me a priestly kingdom and a holy nation.
> (Exodus 19.5–6)

It is the vocation of the covenant community as a whole to maintain the right order rooted in creation, in sharp contrast to Pharaoh's lonely and autocratic rule. Unlike elsewhere at the time, the whole people are responsible for upholding the law and for the administration of justice. All of them together are God's covenant partners. Leaders do have special responsibilities that recognize the reach of their power, and the risks of abusing it, but that responsibility is shared with others, and leaves no get-out clause for standing by when injustice happens. There is immense dignity in inviting the entire community to take part in maintaining justice:

it proclaims their fundamental equality through shared moral responsibility, and sets a pattern of community partnership and accountability. Even where communities are powerless to change their own circumstances, they have a responsibility for the way in which they treat others, particularly those even less fortunate than them (something particularly salient in the New Testament, for instance in 1 Peter).

The official sharing of responsibility to the entire community is a (partial) safeguard against the reality of abuses of power by leaders and possible corruption in the justice system. These abuses are condemned harshly throughout Scripture, whether it is evil kings in Israel, bad shepherds in Ezekiel, or, moving to the New Testament, Pharisees and scribes who add burdens to those already struggling. It is the whole community's duty to discern injustice, to refuse to participate in unjust patterns, and to speak up. Speaking is only a small part of the picture, however – the people of God are called to practise justice, in noticeable and distinctive ways.

New Testament teaching on justice echoes all we have heard already: supporting those in need, providing for basic necessities, hospitality to strangers and care far beyond the household of faith for strangers, widows and orphans, for prisoners and those who are mistreated. The book of Acts stresses the witness of a community that takes care of its vulnerable members, so that 'there was no needy person among them' (Acts 4.34), and caring for the poor is often taken as a mark of Christian character (Tabitha, Cornelius). The goal of these communities was not so much equalization of possessions or resources, as the elimination of need. Care is encouraged within the community, beyond the community and between communities, so that when the church in Jerusalem struggles, Paul encourages churches in Corinth and Rome to have special collections for them. To care is proactive, and applies to those who are far as well as those who are near, literally and metaphorically. Borders and difference are no barrier to the call for justice and compassionate care in the New Testament, which implicitly places a burden on communities to keep finding out what need is present, and how other communities are doing. This care sounds wonderful in theory, but, as always, struggles to express itself in practice. In a world where we have access to endless information about virtually every part of the world, we simply cannot respond to all aspects of need we encounter. How do we balance our different priorities and the calls on our time and resources? Are our choices of where to lend support biased in many ways? How do we seek justice in ways that go beyond the material?

The Church of England, the church I am writing from, is part of a worldwide Communion, where the average Anglican is a young black woman likely to have experienced extreme poverty and/or lived in an area of armed conflict and experienced displacement. How do we work for justice together, in ways that take seriously the responsibilities and historical accountability of our churches? It is easy in debates and conversations in England to forget the Communion, or to dismiss their concerns about our decisions as irrelevant. Yet the vision of Scripture is that we have a claim on one another, and that we are to pursue justice together. Just as the pursuit of justice is always a communal enterprise, rather than the task of individuals only, it is the task of churches together, rather than in isolated communities, locally or nationally.

To pursue justice brings us into almost inevitable conflict. It is relatively easy to have a collection to help Christians abroad and send it as a gift, and feel good about ourselves (and it is right to share our resources); but it is more difficult for the Western Church to consider how its position has made it wealthier than Global South churches, in ways that have been unjust. There has been much discussion of the Black Lives Matter movement, and the need for churches to acknowledge their historic role as part of nations that promoted slavery and the exploitation of other countries. Unsurprisingly, Christians in England disagree on how they need to understand this, how to do justice in historical perspective, and how they assess fairly the role of Christians in the past. Whatever one says about the past, however, there are vast disparities in wealth today, based on historical developments; some Christians are struggling while others live in relative ease. Furthermore, Christians do not live in a separate state, but live within nations that, through their history, policies and involvement in international agreements, contribute to the maintenance of inequality. What kind of claim does this place on Western churches, in responding to distress and struggle across the world, in identifying unjust structures and patterns that contribute to ongoing inequality, and working towards change? We cannot rewrite the past, and may have limited power to influence international trade, armed conflicts and widespread displacement, yet we can be moved by compassion, change what is within our power, and witness to what is beyond our power. We can also resolve to set aside theoretical argument and see the other, listen to their stories and struggles, stand in solidarity, and make space for them to define solutions, and accept the claims they may have upon us for today.

Nurturing just communities

The overwhelming witness of Scripture, from Genesis to Revelation, is that just communities do not simply happen; they are formed, through conscious, intentional and patient work. The deep insight of Exodus, Leviticus and Deuteronomy is that communities, families and households are places where moral virtues, character and imagination are shaped in ways that do – or do not – foster justice. This formation is rooted in story and context; it is never disembodied or purely theoretical, but rests on the interrelation of narratives, tradition and practices. Deuteronomy constantly instructs the people to remember and tell the stories of God's actions in the past, so they can shape the people's life in a new land, with new challenges, new opportunities and new insights. Stories and tradition give us words for articulating the present, inspiration, and confidence in how God works. Deuteronomy stresses the importance of individual and group practices and rituals that help keep the stories, traditions and imagination alive.

The story of Exodus, which extends into the giving of the law, is a story of deep formation: it starts with brokenness, moves to liberation and inspiring divine action, then to the deconstruction of a destructive imagination and the putting in place new ways of being in the pain of the desert. Formation is not easy, and the people's journey is one that brings them face to face with who they are – cherished and loved by God, yet also sinful and steeped in the beliefs of Egypt's economy of scarcity and productivity. The journey also brings them face to face with who God is: compassionate, a God of justice and liberation, yet not a tame God who bends to their desires, but a holy God. The formation of the people is a formation into holiness, bringing together worship and God's passionate compassion for the vulnerable. It is this meeting with truth in all its forms, about themselves and God, that makes it possible for the people to move forward and be shaped by both justice and mercy, as their life together begins and ends with their response of awe and gratitude to God's gift of justice.

Questions for reflection

1 What might Jubilee laws for today look like?
2 How do you decide what causes or projects to contribute to?
3 What parts of the worldwide Church are you well aware of, and what parts might you need to find out more about? Could you commit yourself to praying regularly for a part of the world you know little about right now?

Living in a broken world

Laws in the Bible were not ideal laws – they shaped and reshaped people to think in different ways, and pointed towards an ideal that remained largely out of reach. The life of the people of God is lived in this constant tension, between what God is doing with us now, and what has not yet come, but we are looking towards. Holding a vision for the 'not yet' enables hope, but also shapes how we live in the 'now': when we pray, 'your kingdom come, your will be done', we pray for the 'not yet' to burst into 'now' and transform it. The vocation of the people of God is to live well in this in-between time, and recognize that their vocation in the world is to embody something of the 'not yet' within the constraints of this present world, and, often, with only a clouded vision of what lies ahead.

Many laws in the Old Testament illustrate this principle; they point to something better, yet are realistic for the people now, and incorporate a measure of grace. In a discussion on divorce, Jesus states that the law of Moses was given as an accommodation for the people's 'hardness of heart' (Matthew 9.3–12); this highlights the discrepancy between ideal and reality, and how the law made space for grace, without losing a sense of what to aim for. In very different ways, many of the laws and codes about living in households, both in Old and New Testaments, were written in worlds that took patriarchy, hierarchy and slave ownership as givens. Yet the laws consistently limit the freedom of (male) heads of household and place heavy responsibilities on them to ensure that the poor and weak are treated well.

Laws today still do this – they take some of our beliefs and attitudes for granted, even if those distort our ability to live justly. A frequent saying in the Probation Service was that the state gained more from benefits that remain unclaimed by people entitled to them than it lost in benefit fraud. In many cases that I and others came across, those who had resorted to fraud were actually legally entitled to more (but different) benefits than those they had claimed – but the complexity of the system was such that they took (unethical) shortcuts. Laws and systems fight benefit fraud, and it is often mentioned in the news. To take a benefit you are not entitled to is heavily stigmatized, and punished. And yet, at the other end of the spectrum, there are multiple schemes that make space for tax evasion, some obviously illegal, others internationally sanctioned ways to avoid contributing to society in proportionate and fair ways. The sums of money involved in tax evasion are incomparably larger than those involved in benefit fraud. Yet somehow, the level of stigma, the availability of loopholes and the effort expanded do not reflect the differential. What does this contrasting approach say about our values as a society, and what we take for granted, even as it distorts our ability to do justice and live compassionately?

A key debate in increasingly diverse and multicultural societies is the lack of agreement on what is 'good', hence disputes about what is 'just'. The Church is not immune to these: conflict within the Anglican Communion around sexuality embodies these disagreements, their rootedness in different cultural contexts and their interaction with faith traditions and their interpretation. When societies try to make laws, rules for living life together, the debate cuts right to the heart of these differences: does a just society or community require a common vision, or should we allow people to have as much freedom as possible to live according to their definition/vision of a good life? If we go for a common vision, then whose vision prevails, and why? If we allow maximum freedom, how do we define legitimate moral limits? And in both cases, how do we balance respect for cultural and religious diversity with our duty of care towards one another? Wrestling with these questions embodies Obama's comment on justice as a record of nations or communities 'arguing with their conscience'.

Searching for justice and peace in South Sudan

The following story comes from the country of South Sudan, told by Anglican bishop Anthony Poggo. It explores the struggle to establish a good enough system, and how the Church has lived its vocation within it.

South Sudan came into existence as an independent nation on 9 July 2011, after many years of war between the southern part of the then Sudan and successive regimes of the Sudan. One of the main issues that caused conflicts was religion; the northern part of the then Sudan predominately followed Islam and the southern, Christianity and traditional African religions.

The new independent country went to war within two years of its independence. Contributing factors included the fact that many South Sudanese did not see any tangible impact from independence: ongoing lack of schools, adequate medical services, physical infrastructure, clean drinking water, electricity, lack of all-weather roads. There was no mechanism to stop corruption or land grabbing witnessed by the poor and ordinary people. They had nowhere to turn to, as they had no confidence in the judicial system; some of them turned to other methods to seek their own justice, including the use of guns. It was a fertile ground for disgruntled soldiers and easy for many of these people to join the war in 2013.

Sudan had already suffered through two periods of civil war, between 1955 and 1972, and 1983–2005, with 2.2 million losing their lives and 4.5 million displaced, either as refugees in other countries or internally within Sudan. South Sudanese were marginalized and not offered equitable civil service positions after Sudan's independence. Successive regimes in Khartoum neglected providing resources for the development of the southern part of the country and treated the people of South Sudan with contempt. The main plan they had for the southern part of Sudan was to subjugate the people; they also pursued strategic plans for the 'Arabization and Islamization' of the southern Sudan. With such injustices, there could be no peace in the whole country.

The 1972 Addis Ababa Peace Agreement ushered in an autonomous regional government for the southern region. During this time, southern Sudan experienced a period of relative peace and some basic development took place.

However, South Sudan was refused powers to address judiciary issues. The Khartoum government was keen to maintain Islam (Sharia Law) for the whole country. President Jaafar Nimeiry established harsher forms of Sharia, which included flogging, amputation of hands and feet and criminalization of alcohol consumption.

In 1983 southern Sudanese soldiers staged a mutiny in Bor, partly in response to the gradual abrogation of the 1972 agreement, the imposition of Islamic Sharia (Law) and the change to Arabic instead of English as a language of instruction. This second civil war came to an end in 2005 with the signing of the Comprehensive Peace Agreement (CPA).

The army had fought for a secular Sudan where each Sudanese would have the right of citizenship regardless of religion or race, and to put an end to the policy of Islamization and Arabization. It was a war against injustice as the southern Sudanese people had not experienced justice and peace ever since the nation of the Sudan came into existence. The reality was that Sudanese Muslims and Christians coexisted well with each other. Problems arose when certain politicians used religion to cause division between ordinary people, encouraging some to feel that they were more important in society to achieve political gain.

A key part of the Comprehensive Peace Agreement was the right to self-determination, which led to a referendum after a transitional period of six years. When the people of South Sudan voted in 2011, they overwhelmingly chose independence.

The Church played an important role in ensuring that the referendum took place in time and worked hard to encourage peace and reconciliation among groups fighting each other. In the late 1990s, the New South Sudan Council of Churches facilitated a series of meetings designed to bring together different groups to overcome their internal conflicts, such as the Wunlit Peace and Reconciliation Conference, in 1999, aimed at two major South Sudanese tribes, the Dinka and the

Nuer. The NSCC gathered influential chiefs and elders from both tribes. The participants took many days to share the stories of what they experienced. This is the way we do it in many parts of Africa, listening and allowing each other time. Local ways of resolving conflict are important and should not be disregarded and replaced by time-bound Western models of reconciliation and peace. This conference made a considerable contribution to the unity of South Sudanese factions and subsequent peace talks.

After independence, some inter-tribal conflicts continued to simmer. Tribalism, nepotism and corruption continued on a larger scale than before. Because the government of South Sudan was now in charge of its oil revenue, the government was getting a lot of money and some people were taking advantage of poor governance and accountability systems and diverting some of the income for personal use.

There were complaints of larger tribes dominating smaller tribes. When the new administration was formed, most of the soldiers were from the Dinka community, and accused of tribalism and domination. Some leaders were accused of accumulating power and resources for themselves. The non-Dinka tribes continued to raise concerns over ethnically motivated discrimination in all aspects of government.

By the time of the 2018 peace agreement, the conflict which started in December 2013 had cost over 400,000 lives with 2.5 million people displaced.

An important chapter of the peace agreement is devoted to transitional justice with the aim of promoting reconciliation and accountability for the crimes committed during the 2013–18 war. However, at the time of writing, close to one year later, nothing has been implemented. Many refugees and internally displaced people are carefully monitoring the implementation of the agreement before considering returning to their homes of origin. The question is, is there a political will to implement the entire agreement or are the parties interested in selecting only its palatable aspects?

South Sudan has experienced many challenges since it became a separate country, including how to set up an appropriate judiciary system. The judiciary had always been linked to Khartoum with Arabic as its language. When South Sudan became a separate country and opted to use English, the staff and the judicial system needed to be changed. The issue of language has been a barrier to people receiving efficient judicial services.

Another problem is the lack of independence of the judiciary, and the lack of security of tenure of judges and justices. It is difficult for the average South Sudanese to expect justice in everyday matters, let alone in the issues that have arisen from the 2013 conflict.

Some aspects of South Sudanese culture exacerbate conflict. One of these is vengeance. Many of our cultures in South Sudan encourage or even promote revenge. In some tribes, you are meant to pay back or kill someone from the family, clan or community of someone who killed your kith and kin. In the Kuku language, we have sayings that promote paying back or vengeance for your relatives regardless of whether they are right or wrong. I have seen this whenever someone is accused of wrongdoing or corruption: their community will support them. The thinking is that even if they were a bad person, they still belong to the community. Such cultural practices are a hindrance to justice.

The Bible tells us that '"Vengeance is mine, I will repay" says the Lord.' (Romans 12.19). The reality about vengeance is that it promotes a cycle of violence which it cannot end. The Church has an important role in teaching and encouraging reconciliation and addressing cultural practices that encourage vengeance.

Peace means different things to different people. I was once asked how I would define peace in South Sudan. My immediate response was that peace to me is when I can sit under my mango tree in Kajo-Keji without any fear of attacks from the national army or any other group who took up arms. It is when I can collect food from my own garden as I have had no interruption to the season of cultivation and no cattle or goats are roaming around being herded by herders with AK-47 guns, perhaps with the owner of these cattle sitting somewhere in Juba or other parts of South Sudan.

At the time of writing, what I have described above is still a long way off. Peace and justice are still a long way off. Many people do not have the confidence to settle back in their villages as some of the issues that led them to flee from their homes of origin have not been settled.

Questions for reflection

1 How does this story touch on the themes emerging from our study so far?
2 How does this story connect with you personally and with your church community? What gives you hope in this story?
3 What questions would you want to ask? How might you pray?

When justice fails

In the imagination of Scripture, seeking justice is a constant vocation, yet the human condition is characterized by a chronic failure of justice. That is why laws and a judicial system are necessary, because injustice is characteristic of sin, and sin touches all human beings, their systems and institutions. To be grounded in Christianity is therefore to be grounded in an unflinchingly honest view of ourselves and our abilities, our limitations and blind spots. Scripture calls us to live well even when justice fails. One of the responses, as we have already touched on, is to take a prophetic stand and speak out against injustice. Another is to nurture communities of justice where we learn how to practise justice. And yet – what happens when all this is done, but there is still no justice to be found, and injustice bites deep?

The letter of 1 Peter, in the New Testament, is written in this kind of context. Peter addresses the dispersed communities of believers throughout Asia Minor, consistently marginalized and harassed for their faith. They experience injustice and oppression on a daily basis, and have little power to stand against their oppressors. Many are women and slaves, and even the free men have low social status due to their faith. Peter's words to them are extraordinary. They are full of warmth and affection, sketch out the depth of God's love and care for them, and counteract their sense of being disregarded or abandoned. Peter starts by helping them to see themselves through God's eyes, rather than through the eyes of their oppressors, using the words and concepts found in Exodus and Leviticus as the people of Israel were learning to be God's people, rather than Pharaoh's: 'But you are a chosen race, a royal priesthood, a holy nation, God's own people, in order that you may proclaim the mighty acts of him who called you out of darkness into his marvellous light' (1 Peter 2.9).

Peter does not tell the believers to rise up and revolt or fight back – and we may find this difficult; what Peter does is give them a sense of their value, tools for survival, and lay on them obligations which may be beyond their strength. There are many different types of responses to injustice in Scripture, Exodus being only one. God always works towards justice, but how this work takes place looks and feels different in different contexts. Peter here encourages Christians to be an alternative community, whose life together is so radically different that it challenges the habits and values of the Roman Empire. He tells them to 'honour everyone' in the same sentence as he counsels 'honour the emperor' (2.17). In other words – treat everyone as worthy of honour and respect, not just the emperor, as would have been the custom. Roman society was heavily hierarchical, and slaves not only had little power, but were often considered not to have moral faculties. Yet Peter addresses them first, and treats them as full human beings, with a conscience and a responsibility to do good, and enjoins them to actively and courageously persevere in virtue. The very way in which Peter writes to a community under duress challenges the imagination of the Empire, and begins the process of constructing a different, alternative imagination that resists the prevailing trend.

Injustice, however, does not always direct itself at groups defined by personal or social characteristics. The following story is of one person's unsuccessful search for justice, and their response as a Christian. It is not meant as an example or a template for others. Rather it is offered (anonymized with identifying details changed) as a story to enter into, to help us think, ask questions, and stand in solidarity and witness. You may find this story upsetting as it contains references to abuse, and therefore may want to skip this part of the chapter.

Anya's story

I grew up with every privilege you can imagine. My school friends envied me and thought I was so lucky. We had money, a big house, nice cars, lots of holidays, posh furniture, all the latest gadgets. A girl who came to my house once to pick up some homework said, 'You've got everything, you have. You've got everything!' In material terms that's true. And when it comes to lots of other privileges, that's true too – race, class, education, health, everything was on my side. The problem is that all of that made it so much harder to see what was behind closed doors. The way that I flinched and protected my face whenever my mother walked past. The secret places to hide for hours if my dad was on a rampage. The constant humiliations and beatings, and the other stuff. The stuff you can't talk about, that makes you sick in the pit of your stomach. I had a friend I talked to for a bit, and we used to compare bruises, have a kind of competition on how we'd been beaten that week – hand, fist, belt, stick. But I never told her the really bad stuff. She never told me more than the beatings. I wonder whether there was more for her too. We did compare notes on siblings – trying to protect the little ones, and trying to get the older ones to take the blame for what was wrong that day, even if neither of us had actually done anything in the first place. There was no logic anyway.

I tried to tell a teacher, but she hit me for telling lies, and told my parents. You can imagine what happened next. When I was a teenager, I tried to tell my GP, but he'd gone to medical school with my mother, so he didn't believe it. Other people in the family knew what was going on, but they were scared too. My parents didn't groom people, they just scared them. And from the outside, we were the perfect family, respected in the community. I told a friend, and his parents, but they didn't know what to do. Children have overactive imaginations, you know. Why believe them?

I buried it all deep, and lived the life I was supposed to live. Privileged, perfect. Dying inside. Things have changed in 50 years. There are lots of stories around about safeguarding, and child protection, and believing victims, so I spoke up. I thought that telling my story might do something, maybe protect someone else, or help me feel better. It didn't. I spoke up, and people believed me, but in the end, when I spoke to the police, they dropped the case. I had to tell my story three times before something started to be done, and it all came to nothing. I put myself on the line, and nothing happened.

What do I do with that? I have pondered a lot what justice means. I'm not sure what I was looking for from the police. I think I wanted validation for my story. I wanted someone to say, 'It really happened and we're sorry. It shouldn't have, and we will make the world a better place.' I wanted justice, but I don't really know what 'justice' would look like after the facts. Justice means having a normal childhood, not having to go through any of this, ever. Nobody can repair or repay what I have lost. I had to learn to live with injustice, because that's all I had.

I'm a Christian, and that didn't always help. People and pastors have reacted in different ways – some of them have held me as I cried, prayed with me, walked with me, and the best of them haven't expected me to ever say, it's better. Some of them have been rubbish and said stupid things, mostly because my story scares them. If it happened to me, then it could happen to anyone, and the justice system could fail them, too. People find it hard when they can't actually do anything to change things. Some also said I should forgive. I don't really know what that means. I have seen a therapist and learnt to live with the trauma – I don't have the nightmares and the flashbacks I used to have. I don't think about it all every day like I used to, it doesn't define who I am. I don't live in the past, so if forgiveness is about becoming free from the gnawing anger and resentment and endless yearning for things to have been different, then maybe I have forgiven.

I am not angry with my parents, most of the time; I don't want revenge. But the consequences of what they did keep catching up with me. I think I'm OK, and then things happen – enter a relationship, kids getting to an age that reminds me of stuff, lose someone I love, or smaller things, what someone says or does when I don't expect it, and I am back there, in the pain. Or I realize that I am reacting in a way that's twisted, or unhelpful, and I see a new side to the damage they did me. Forgiveness is a never-ending thing. I have to go back to asking the question again and again, not because I hold on to yesterday's pain, but because today brings fresh pain with alarming regularity. And I have to forgive myself for not being magically better. I used to be angry – at my parents, my siblings, my family. At everybody who knew and did nothing, the teachers, the doctors, my friends. I'm not angry any more, because I know that they just couldn't cope with what they heard, and so it was easier to deny, or ignore, or pretend it wasn't there. And in the end, it wasn't their fault anyway. They could have done better, but I wonder whether I could have done better too, with siblings, or friends, or people I don't even realize I failed. I'm not excusing not acting in the face of injustice, just saying, I understand how it happens.

I pray for them all. That's the only way forward I have found, and I give myself a break when I have a bad day. I try to look around me and see what other people miss, try and be aware that people have back stories few others know, I remind myself that you never know what happens in someone's home, or their heart. I tried to understand how my parents came to do the things they did; not to excuse them, but to try and be fair. To gauge their responsibility somehow. I know from bitter experience that the ways in which I was hurt have twisted some of my reactions, and my ability to relate. It is true for them too. And yet at the same time, I wonder, what made them go that step further? How do people step from regular sin into pure evil? And what are we supposed to do with them? Even if they had gone to prison, I think I would still be asking the same questions, and I would still have no answer.

Retribution wouldn't help me, even though I think they should be held accountable. The only thing I really want is for them to understand the horror of what they've done, really feel it in their bones. I'm not sure anything else would be justice. I get angry with God too. Some days I think he is there, holding me and healing me. Some days I wonder whether he is anywhere at all. And if he is around somewhere, where on earth was he back then? And at the same time, I couldn't live without God. It's my lifeline. Some people call it a crutch. I don't care. God and my church have kept my head above water, and that's what matters. I ask questions that have no answer, and all I get back, like Job, is the sense that God is there and bigger than it all. And that justice really is a thing, and I need to keep going after it, because without the constant search, what's left?

Questions for reflection

1 Have you, or someone close to you, had an experience of justice denied, or impossible justice? How does this make you feel? How do you pray (or not) about it?
2 Do you think it is always possible or right to forgive?
3 Think of an instance of continuing, long-term injustice, maybe from the news. Where is God in all that? How might you pray?

Prayer

This chapter has explored the gap between the world as it is, and the world we are longing for. Many projects seek to live out justice in a broken world; one of them, the Community of the Cross of Nails, works for reconciliation worldwide, and encourages its members to pray the following prayer, a confession and petition for change.

The Coventry Litany of Reconciliation

All have sinned and fallen short of the glory of God.

The hatred which divides nation from nation, race from race, class from class,
Father forgive.

The covetous desires of people and nations to possess what is not their own,
Father forgive.
The greed which exploits the work of human hands and lays waste the earth,
Father forgive.

Our envy of the welfare and happiness of others,
Father forgive.

Our indifference to the plight of the imprisoned, the homeless, the refugee,
Father forgive.

The lust which dishonours the bodies of men, women and children,
Father forgive.

The pride which leads us to trust in ourselves and not in God,
Father forgive.

Be kind to one another, tender hearted, forgiving one another, as God in Christ forgave you.[2]

---

2   From <http://coventrycathedral.org.uk/ccn/the-coventry-litany-of-reconciliation/>, copyright © 2021 The Community of the Cross of Nails.

4

Justice and incarnation

Restoring the image of God

Everything we have considered so far shows that within a Christian, scriptural imagination, justice is incarnational, rooted in time and place, and profoundly interpersonal. Justice is linked to the foundational stories of Genesis, of human beings being made in the image of God, and this image being degraded by sin. As brokenness and sin enter the world, the image of God becomes twisted, and human beings both think of themselves as more than they are and treat others as less than they are. Sin and injustice damage our intrinsic humanity, our reflection of the image of God, our personhood. To seek justice is to work to restore this image and enable it to flourish.

The centrality of the Incarnation

The stories of creation in Genesis 1 and 2 portray abundant life, the kind of life Jesus later promises his followers in John 10.10, 'I came that they may have life, and have it abundantly.' To get a true, undistorted picture of 'abundant life', however, we need to look at God himself, the source of the 'image', or we are at risk of fashioning an idol, an idea of abundant life based on human desires and values, shaped by the wider economy of scarcity and surrounding cultures. Desires and cultures are not necessarily wrong, but they are partial, a mix of good and bad, whose value needs discerning in dialogue with Scripture and the Spirit. In the Old Testament, God walked patiently with his people, intimately involved with Israel to help them discern and embody justice and compassion. In the New Testament, God takes this walking with humanity further: in the words of John's Gospel, 'the Word became flesh and lived among us' (John 1.14); the Greek words actually say, 'the Word became flesh and pitched a tent among us', a turn of phrase that beautifully captures the fragility and transience of humanity.

Much of the Old Testament had focused on enabling the people of God to live out their vocation of justice and righteousness. The Incarnation stands within this overall arc of covenantal, close relationship and formation of communities. The coming of Christ cannot be reduced to the cross and resurrection, and salvation accomplished on behalf of humanity. It is the whole of Jesus' life that matters, and one of the ways it matters is through its incarnation of justice. It is in watching the interaction of Jesus with other human beings, his response to their culture and personal attributes, his emotional involvement with the pain of the world, that we see justice at work. Justice is essentially incarnational.

It is odd therefore that when philosophers and theologians speak of justice, they often try to do it in dis-incarnated ways, away from specific people and contexts, away from real bodies that live and love and suffer. They may talk of a 'typical' or 'ideal' human. Judicial systems themselves are based on an idea of a 'juridical person', a typical human with their rights and responsibilities, and a 'common man' who can judge what is reasonable. Yet there is no 'typical human'; all human beings have a story, a place, a time, a culture, that have shaped them and their choices. Generalizations can – and need to – be made, to ensure a minimum level of justice; but for *full* justice to happen in practice, real people must be met, and heard. A society cannot be just unless it enables each and every person to be seen and heard, rather than shielded by the trappings of status and power, or hidden by discrimination and oppression.

When I worked in the Probation Service, I wrote countless pre-sentence reports. These were composed after someone was found guilty, but before an exact sentence was handed down. A guilty verdict set the parameters within which a sentence (meant for punishment, public protection, rehabilitation, compensation and deterrence) was defined. There is a certain amount of leeway to define how to best achieve these multiple goals. Some of the leeway rests on the circumstances of the offence, degree of intent, aggravating features, and assessment of future risk. But a pre-sentence report also tries to give a sense of the person behind the offence. I met with offenders, and listened to their stories. Some were exaggerated, but most were corroborated by external sources. Almost always, they were sad stories of traumatic childhoods, intergenerational dysfunction, combinations of various disadvantages, together with conscious decisions and distorted thinking. Often there were deep-seated mental health challenges. Those I was reporting on had already been found guilty, so guilt and responsibility were not in question. What *was* in question was, who is this person? How have they got to where they are now? How much is their sole responsibility, and how much needs to be borne by others – parents, friends, carers, communities, institutions, wider society? How do we respond to this person humanely, in ways that will help restore the image of God often so shattered within them?

It is sometimes difficult for victims and those affected by evil acts to consider that this exploration of a person is part of 'justice'. It is not retribution. But it does belong to justice on a larger canvas, because it touches on questions of what kind of society we want to be, and how we can enable every person to flourish. The prison system is exorbitantly expensive, and therefore most offenders will one day be released. To seek to meet them as people is to ask how they can be supported to take their place within a just society, given their history, limitations and proper responsibilities. Even if people could be kept behind bars for ever, prisons themselves are communities, with complex interpersonal relationships. Therefore we need to ask how they can be just and foster 'abundant life' within their restrictions, for this is part of seeing another person's humanity as irreducible.

When I trained as a probation officer, in the first week of training, our cohort was asked: 'True justice always holds the quality of mercy. Discuss.' The discussion was hugely polarized, and the group passionately divided. Is mercy additional to justice, something we might choose to do, but ultimately is not just or required? Or is mercy intrinsic to justice? If we consider judicial matters in isolation, it may be possible to argue that justice needs to be impartial and that mercy needs to come from without the system. If we consider justice more widely however, at the level of entire societies, justice and mercy need to walk hand in hand: true justice must consider the responsibility of an entire society in shaping its members, and recognize that there is always something in the 'other' that we do not know, and things within ourselves that we hide or deny. For true justice to be served, there needs to be a space for mercy, so that the fallibility and brokenness of all humanity can be held, including those being judged and those doing the judging. To hold justice and mercy together is to attend to the reality of our common humanity.

Darren's story

Before we explore this any further, I would like you to meet Darren Howie, who kindly agreed to share his story.

> I grew up in the heart of a working-class Scottish town. It gave me the quintessential baptism into a world of crime and addiction. I was the product of a broken home, which in turn was the by-product of a town devastated by post-industrial

Thatcherism and a community and wider family decimated by crime and substance abuse. I started experimenting with substances in my early teens, introduced to solvents by peers in the care system, then progressing to harder drugs. My drug-taking was an attempt to feel something beyond myself and to escape the misery of my poverty-stricken town. I also took drugs to rebel against a system that seemed to be against people like me. Drug-taking, and the rave culture I embraced, was a tribal entity and protest act. It was a lot of fun to begin with and we felt strong relational bonds and a deep sense of connection and shared purpose. However, this was partially drug induced and would begin to fragment and turn sour as our mental well-being became seriously compromised due to the nasty side-effects of regular pill-popping.

In my late teens I became embroiled in criminal activity, primarily to fund drugs, but also because it was exciting. Entering the young offenders institution as a 17-year-old kid was basically promotion, confirmation that I'd 'arrived'. But it was a subtle yet sinister reminder that I was a 'menace to society', part of the world's problems that needed to be 'fixed'. Prison became something of an occupational hazard, a revolving door between incarceration and liberation, between hunger, homelessness and heroin and three square meals a day, a roof over my head, and a life-saving methadone programme. Intravenous heroin abuse was my life for well over a decade and there seemed to be no way out, no hope for me. I had no hope for the future, and my heart got harder and more twisted in the world that I'd partially created for myself – it was bent against the world, people and myself. After years of reflecting on my past, I've come to the conclusion that I didn't just commit crimes for fun, or to get money to score drugs. I believe it was also down to a subconscious desire to use my creativity, my brain, my abilities. Being a criminal requires a certain amount of imagination, savvy and people skills. It came as a surprise to me in later years that I was highly intelligent, a gifted person, full of hidden potential, though it was all grossly misdirected.

I struggle to recall a time when someone who represented the system (social services, mainstream education, juvenile detention) noticed my worth, never mind helped me to nurture and re-channel my creative energy. Though there was a brief spell in my early teens when I was at Ballikinrain Castle List D (a children's home run by the Church of Scotland), where I felt valued and began to flourish due to the love and support of the staff. However, it was short lived, and I was swallowed up by the social and cultural problems of my home town once again. My time at the Castle came to an abrupt and disastrous end as the local authority attempted to reintegrate me into mainstream education. I believe the system failed me, and sadly it's still failing people like me. Those with power failed to acknowledge the complex story of my youth and address the trauma-induced lifestyle of a hurting young man. Those who were charged with my care – close family, social workers, police officers, dual diagnosis, or probation officers – struggled to help me unpack or understand my shame, rejection or anger. The system failed to recognize, acknowledge or even name these powerful emotions as triggers for anti-social behaviour.

A lot can happen in 20 years. It all began to change for me in 2002. During my last ever prison sentence, ironically for a crime I didn't commit (a first for me), a prison chaplain came into my cell and told me I was going to die if I didn't accept help soon. It was a kind of epiphany moment. He spoke life to me: 'It doesn't have to be like this, you're better than your choices, your behaviour is not who you are, you are loved, you are important, and you are unique.' The God that he represented, the Christian God who is fully revealed in and through Jesus Christ, a God who enters right into the heart of our human misery and mess, had a message for me: I was of supreme worth. The chaplain's face was the face of a kind and gracious power and authority that I had never known. I wanted out of that cell and the hell of the life I was living. He offered me a brief glimpse of hope despite and beyond it. When all the props of life had apparently gone, God came to me in the face of another human being. It was in that moment that true justice was about to be served, which for me is really all about forgiveness. I felt that freedom had arrived. The prison of my mind, the confinement of my will, and the cage my heart was in were more incarcerating than the punitive system I was stuck in. A greater freedom awaited, if I wanted it.

A new chapter in my story had begun, but I had a long way to travel. My son, only eight, had found me six weeks previously with a belt round my neck trying to hang myself. I'd been in utter despair. I was ashamed of the person I'd become, a six-and-a-half stone heroin addict with no friends and a family who didn't want to know me. How was I ever going to wade through the physical, emotional and psychological debris of the tsunami that was my life? Even though I didn't have to accept the life I was living, I'd be lying if I said I wasn't terrified and overwhelmed. It was a bittersweet juncture on my road to recovery. This sense of liminality is echoed by others who've attempted to leave their 'old life' behind, like Jimmy Boyle, the former lifer and ex-Glasgow gangster who said, 'I became an alien to my past, yet I felt like a stranger in my future.'

But there's power in hope. It's amazing how the power of encountering the kindness of another human being, called and sent by the Spirit of God, has the potential to radically alter the course of another person's life. This is the one good thing the system did for me: appoint chaplains. However, I'm more inclined to believe that God triumphed where the system failed. There's power in people, too. On my release, the chaplain got me into a 12-month, faith-based, residential rehabilitation community, where I encountered more of this God and found a home to call my own. Deep down this is what I longed for, though I never knew it back then: a loving family, a welcome embrace, a place to belong, a place to contribute: community.

There, I began to challenge and reject the labels that society had placed on me, such as 'once a smackhead always a smackhead'. There, I had the first glimpse of my true worth, my true self, the innocent little boy who'd been bruised by the world and forced to survive. The first church I was a member of had life-givers and people who were there for me when I needed them the most. People who weren't put off by the messiness of ministering among reforming drug addicts or ex-offenders, or fazed by regular relapses in the early days. They were people who had the gift of grace and mercy in abundance.

I learned to trust others in the church community. I was also given responsibility. People trusted me. I even learned to love others, which was an alien concept, even though I still struggled to love myself. I learned that there are good people in the world and that I don't have to question or measure people's worth or genuineness based on my own negative experiences. An old schoolteacher who I've been reconciled with once said to me, 'You simply became the monster that we treated you like.' I say all this without dismissing my own responsibility to change my ways. God in isolation did not offer or provide enough power or tools to keep me from stumbling on the journey. I needed people. It was impossible to do it alone. I needed compassion, kindness and grace, most of which the systems and authorities lacked. This is why faith-based rehabs like the one I was in, and the diverse Christian community I belonged to afterwards, are vital. They create safe spaces for trust to grow and grace to be practised. Churches need to take risks with people like me. The gospel demands it.

I was transformed by being a part of a radical community of belonging. The people of my church community, who welcomed me into their lives – not just two hours on a Sunday – were also transformed. The 'us and them' categories that plagued our subcultures slowly disintegrated. Peter was no longer just Peter the copper, our local bobby, he was Peter my friend who I played football with every week. Arthur was no longer just Arthur the headmaster of the local high school, he was Arthur my mentor and spiritual dad. The 'addict' and 'criminal' will only ever be fully transformed when the society in which they live is willing and committed to being transformed in the process. People like me can become a part of the solution to the world's problems and not just the cause.

If you'd told me back then that I'd become a messenger of God, I'd have laughed in your face. If you'd told me I'd be a key-holder at HMP Nottingham, working with probation and chaplaincy, and running a coffee-roasting company that supports disenfranchised people, I wouldn't have believed you. If you'd told me that I would have three lively, lovely children, I'd have probably freaked out and run a mile. If you'd told me that I'd hold a first-class postgraduate degree, I'd have called you a rotten liar (or something stronger). If you'd told me back then that I'd be a priest in the Church of England, the most middle-class church in the land, I'd have mocked you and told you to jog on. This is what God's Church is capable of. This is good news.

Questions for reflection

1 Does anything particularly speak to you in Darren's story?
2 What questions or challenges does this story prompt?
3 Do you know – or how could you get to know – someone like Darren?

Learning to see

The turning point of Exodus was the people's crying out, and God *hearing* their cry, and *seeing* their oppression. The theme of seeing the oppressed, the marginalized, the 'other', starts even before Exodus. In Genesis, the story of Hagar proclaims that God is 'El-Roi', that is, 'God of seeing', or 'the God who sees'. Hagar was Sarah's slave girl. When Abraham and Sarah struggled to conceive, Sarah 'gave' her slave to Abraham – so that sexual abuse was added to slavery. Sarah then became jealous of Hagar for becoming pregnant, and Hagar ran away to the desert. God meets her there, unbidden, assures her that God has heard her, and instructs her to name her son Ishmael, which means 'God hears'. Hagar names the place of encounter 'the Well of the Living One who Sees me' and calls God, El-Roi (Genesis 16.7–14). Seeing and hearing are an intrinsic part of addressing injustice.

The woman with a loss of blood and Jairus' daughter

This dual emphasis threads itself throughout Scripture, and is obvious in the ministry of Jesus. One of the stories that show this attentiveness to the whole person, and what lies behind appearances, is the raising of Jairus' daughter and the healing of the woman with a haemorrhage in the key text Mark 5.21–43. Jesus is called by Jairus, a wealthy, well-established man, to heal his dying daughter. An unnamed woman touches Jesus on the way, hoping for healing from chronic bleeding.

This is a story of two halves. One, a story of urgency, of crisis, of acute need, and the other, a story of chronic pain and illness, always present but never urgent. On the surface, it may not be a story of justice. However, there is an inherent unfairness to illness and how it strikes. There is also unfairness in access to treatment, and injustice and discrimination in how those who are affected are treated. Here, time adds to the sense of injustice: it looks as if Jesus cannot heal both women. There is not enough time. What to do? If Jesus does not hurry, the little girl may die. But if Jesus does hurry, the unnamed woman may live, still in pain, struggling, ostracised. Loss of blood made her ceremonially unclean, barred from joining in normal community activities and religious gatherings. On the other hand, a child's life is in the balance. It is an impossible decision. No one can, or should, measure the value of one life against another.

Questions of priorities often shape life-and-death life decisions. however, and have done so most powerfully during the Covid-19 pandemic. Plenty of ink has been spilt critiquing decisions on who to prioritize for treatment, who should access vaccines first, or in what order, who is 'essential' and who isn't, and there have been endless debates around how to balance risks, limitations and freedom. No one (or very few) openly says that one life matters more than another – yet underlying the debates is the sense that if we cannot protect everyone, then we have to construct a hierarchy, which inevitably ranks lives in terms of who is more valuable – and who has most power to influence how the 'list' is ordered.

In our story, most people expect Jesus to attend to the urgent. Jesus, unlike us, has the ability to attend to both. He does not let urgency blind him to other pain and need. He extends the same care and compassion to the woman who is not dying, but whose life has shrunk to unbearable proportions, as to a dying child and her grieving father. The crowd may have expected Jesus to attend to the request of a powerful, highly regarded man like Jairus, rather than to a poor, unnamed, 'unclean' woman. Jairus had all the cards in his hands: male, socially accepted, a religious leader, wealthy, articulate, and confident enough in his own standing to approach Jesus outright. Conversely, the woman is of no consequence or status, with nothing to offer in return for a healing, not even payment, as she has spent all her money looking for a cure. She is alone, powerless, with no resources left, and does not even consider herself worthy to speak to Jesus directly.

Therefore she approaches Jesus from behind, using the crowd as a shield to keep her unseen, unheard and unnoticed. She does not even touch Jesus, just the end of his clothes. She does not seek full human touch – something she would have craved, as her loss of blood has isolated her for so many years. Does she really think things will change? She is so eager not to be seen, not let anyone see her hope, maybe not even to let herself hope, so that if she isn't healed, no one will laugh or condemn her for being part of a crowd who would not want to be touched by her in case she made them unclean too. The crowds could easily turn on her. It is unclear how far the laws on ritual purity were observed (they prescribe quarantine in this case in Leviticus 15.25–30), but the dominant picture is that of a woman brought down by the weight of oppressive social customs applied without care or grace, to the point where her humanity, in her own eyes and those of others, has diminished and become invisible.

She is healed, and may have expected to just go home and quietly burst into tears of joy. Of all people, she would understand the need to attend to the sick little girl quickly. Instead, Jesus does the unexpected, and stops. The urgency of Jairus' request recedes, and Jesus seeks to bring this invisible woman into his sight, and the sight of all those who have shunned her and her pain for years. The disciples are confused, and cannot understand the difference between inadvertent touch in a jostling crowd and intentional, personal touch. Jesus knows. A connection has been made, and he does not leave healing to a disembodied, impersonal action: he recognizes that illness has many ramifications beyond the physical. It creates a narrative, and shapes social belonging in ways that can become oppressive and unjust. Jesus looks, but the woman steps forward. She has choice and agency, despite her fear and trembling. Jairus had initiated encounter with Jesus, but Jesus initiates encounter with the woman. Jairus' primary emotion was anguish for his beloved child, the woman's, fear that she may have trespassed. Both are desperate, aware that Jesus is their last resort, but their desperation is expressed differently according to social status.

The woman tells Jesus 'the whole truth'. What is 'the whole truth'? The truth of the specific moment, or the truth of what her life has been like so far, her desperation, her hope, her faith? The insistence that she tells the whole truth contrasts sharply with her trying to hide before. Now she allows herself to be seen and known by Jesus, and Jesus commends her faith and declares her healed. Proclaiming her healing enables her instantly to be restored as a full member of the community, and removes excuses for others to treat her differentially. To commend her faith goes a step further, and elevates her. She is no longer a diminutive figure, in comparison with a leader of the synagogue. She is a person to be respected and valued. Jesus' actions attend to the whole of her humanity, including hidden needs, and challenge the crowd's perceptions and prejudices.

The rest of the story is equally astonishing. Jairus had run to Jesus with an emergency. He is well known, visible, powerful. He has the right to ask and be heard, and uses it. We know his name, unlike that of either woman. People are interested, and his pain becomes a spectacle for crowds eager to see another miracle. They hadn't been that interested in the woman. She was not spectacle material. Her life was not one others aspire to. The double edge of privilege bites here; privilege gives Jairus access and shortcuts; yet at the same time, he is over-seen, so that his grief and personhood are lost, reduced to spectacle.

Why did Jesus physically go with Jairus? There are accounts of 'remote miracles', such as the healing of the centurion's servant in Matthew 8.5–13. The circumstances are different, but they show that Jesus could have healed the little girl from afar, without delay. Yet he makes Jairus wait, and attends to a woman. This in itself is another challenge to perceptions of worth and social order, and a move towards restoring the proper order of a just community where all are equally valued.

Jesus heals Jairus' daughter, but does it behind closed doors. He doesn't let the crowd follow, not even most of his disciples. He shields those already visible, and refuses to let a child's life be turned into a spectacle. In contrast to the unnamed woman's faith, Jairus' household jeer at the thought that Jesus can raise the girl from death, or a deep coma. Unlike the public declaration of healing in the crowd, Jesus tells the household that 'no one should know this' (Mark 5.43). A high-profile healing could have added to Jairus' status, but the already privileged do not need additional status. The subtext of the episode is that of an equalizing of status, and a challenge to the wider community. They are not given the spectacle they wanted, and instead are invited to change their behaviour towards both unnamed women and Jairus. Jesus is teaching the disciples, and others who may want to learn, to really see, hear and touch: not distractedly, not letting pre-existing prejudices and values cloak the real person before them, but attending to their full humanity, putting compassion and the needs of the other, the suffering other, first. The crowd does not have a claim on the story of Jairus' daughter. But suffering in their midst puts a claim on them to reassess their communal values and habits.

From seeing to doing

This story stands in continuity with the search for overarching justice in the Old Testament. It is practical rather than theoretical, and focuses on attending to marginalized voices and the breaking down of barriers to solidarity and equality. It is the encounter with the woman that brings about something new in the story, as she is revealed as a full person. Encountering someone marginalized, or simply different, other, is essential to developing a robust vision for justice, because it enables correctives, outside perspectives, to challenge and prompt a re-evaluation of what we take for granted. In this story, the true 'other' is not the woman, but Jesus, who disrupts a system of values and social organization with unexpected action and practical love.

Encountering otherness and letting it challenge our own presuppositions is painful and risky. It involves taking a step into the unknown, willingness to explore together rather than being in control. It also means sharing one's convictions without attempting to change the other, but rather listening and being willing to enter into their world view and see ourselves as they see us. This embrace of a journey towards the other does not mean that we have to discard our beliefs and practices, or fall into endless relativism. Rather, it means adopting a posture of listening and openness, and the humility to know that one person's view, one community's view, one culture or subculture's view is never comprehensive, ideal or perfect. It means accepting that we need one another. The parable of the Good Samaritan illustrates the difficulty we have with this journey into otherness in the key text, Luke 10.25–37.

The parable answers the lawyer's question, 'Who is my neighbour?' The perspective we are invited into is that of the man who travels and is attacked by robbers, while the Samaritan is the 'other', the unexpected neighbour. Yet often, when we read this story, we unconsciously switch places and see ourselves in the shoes of the Samaritan, the one who has to help. It is easier to regard ourselves as the person who knows and understands how to love and care for the other, how to do justice, rather than to take Jesus' hint: you, the listener, are not the 'other' who knows what justice and compassion look like. You are the injured man, who needs this other to teach you what a true 'neighbour' is. It is the despised, silenced, shunned Samaritan's voice that is needed to help you grow towards deeper justice.

What would that look like for us today? Whose voices do we need to hear? The parable is an implicit encouragement to attend to those voices and people we do not see, hear or want to touch, and let them teach us. Furthermore, the parable suggests that attending to those voices is not an act of charity, through which we, who are in control, redress the balance of justice. Listening to silenced voices and seeing the invisible enables them to minister to us.

Who is visible or invisible, heard or not, victim or oppressor, self or other, is complex to identify. Some situations are clear; however, people have multiple aspects to their identity and they hold different roles and positions within different networks and contexts, with different degrees of power and control within each. The concept of intersectionality describes how these interconnected aspects of group or individual categorizations create overlapping and interdependent systems of discrimination or disadvantage. If one person embodies several characteristics that make them less visible, valued or heard within a given context, they suffer deeper multiple discrimination, and access to justice is much more difficult. Conversely, the more 'privileges' you have (like Jairus), the more situations occur within which you have power or control. The balance of power and powerlessness, advantage and disadvantage, changes with context and situations. This helps us understand the complexity of all relationships, and how difficult it is to 'do justice', because justice is difficult to achieve in isolation: we need to consider all the different types of interactions that we are involved in communally, and how they overlap and influence one another.

While Scripture places a particular responsibility on the powerful to listen well, the fact is that, however we are positioned in life, there will be some we do not see, or cannot see, or do not want to see, or whose voice we want to silence. There will always be someone who is 'other'. The Good Samaritan story was uncomfortable for everyone in the audience, regardless of their status or power, because of the weight of historical conflict and injustice, the sense of threat and disgust, the disputes on morality, justice and ethics. The deep, deep challenge of the Good Samaritan story is for all of us never to think that we do not need this other we fear or despise or disregard. The parable makes the further point that justice and care for the other can – and should – be extended to the other even when we disagree with them and their beliefs. It is concerned with macro, rather than micro, justice; it aims to help us think of how to build communities that constantly keep themselves open to developing and extending justice further.

Questions for reflection

1 Who comes to mind immediately when you think about justice? Who comes to mind when you think of injustice?
2 How could you find out who may be invisible or unheard in your local community? What about the invisible and unheard in the news, nationally and internationally?
3 Who is 'other' to you? Who might you need to learn to see as a neighbour?

Seeing the big picture

The parable of the Good Samaritan fundamentally challenges the human habit of binary thinking. The tendency to reduce the 'other' to a negative image of ourselves, or to a caricature that forgets their particularity and humanity, is clearly not a new thing. It is, however, a tendency particularly obvious on social media today, as disagreement quickly turns into 'blocking' someone, or mounting a campaign against them. People are reduced to one or two beliefs that clash with prevailing norms, or an individual's own. Sometimes they are reduced to the worst aspect of who they are. Sometimes to just one aspect of their entire life or belief system. Often, they are not allowed to tell their story for themselves, in its nuances and with its own hinterland. Their story is retold by detractors who disagree with it, from without rather than from within. Can justice truly exist if we treat others as less fully human, less complex than ourselves? And how do we hold one another accountable justly, without writing the other off?

The Western world is concerned with justice and discrimination – and this is good. Passion for diversity and equal treatment is deeply consonant with much that we have discussed so far. The additional question to ask, as Christians, and in contribution to wider debates, is *how* we engage in these debates. How do we hold people accountable without becoming arrogant, or superficial in our engagement? How do we humanize every person in a dispute or situation?

The ministry of Jesus consistently brings together accountability and grace. He eats with publicans and Pharisees alike, giving them time and meeting them in homes and domestic spaces. His criticisms of the Pharisees are harsh, but they are not based on non-engagement. They often focus on lack of grace and humility as a key fault. Some of his harshest words are reserved for those who are convinced that they've got it right, that they know what justice and righteousness are, and are ready to condemn others for falling short. It is a lack of humility and grace, and the dismissal of the 'other', that are at issue. Jesus does not say that the law, or their principles are wrong; it is the way in which they see themselves with respect to others that is their failing. Conversely, Jesus also holds those who are disadvantaged and despised to account for their own choices: he tells the woman caught in adultery to 'Go on your way, and from now on do not sin again' (John 8.11), he confronts the Samaritan woman with the truth of her lifestyle (John 4.16–18), Zacchaeus' unjust lifestyle is transformed (Luke 19.1–10), and his first words to a man with a disability lowered through the roof are that his sins are forgiven (Matthew 9.2–7). Jesus is very clear that he has come to call sinners to repent (Luke 5.32), and does not shy away from speaking of the cost of sin and the need for transformation. He does so with both firmness and grace, and humanizes those he talks to. He does not reject them or write them off, but invites them into a better life. The real problem is not those who know they need help, it is those who think that they do not and that others do. Those who thought that they already led good lives tended to disassociate themselves from those they considered deficient. They treated sin as contagious and dangerous for them. Jesus, instead, practised contagious holiness. I often wonder what contagious holiness would look like in the bitter world of current public debates. Binary debates and 'othering' ultimately prevent us from searching for justice and constructing the world together. And if the world is not constructed together, it almost inevitably means that some will be excluded or silenced, and feel aggrieved or unjustly treated, thereby perpetuating a cycle of bitterness and conflict.

Jesus models a completely different approach. If, instead of focusing on micro situations, we look at what God did in Christ, we see Jesus entering the perspective of humanity, in the most complete choice of attending to the reality of the 'other' that can be imagined. Jesus does not condone any of humanity's failings, yet sees life through the eyes of the other as a way towards grace and justice. The option of full incarnation is of course not open to anyone else – but we can choose to reverse perspectives and try and see life through the eyes of the other: their fears, their joys, the influences and circumstances that have shaped them, while nurturing an awareness of our own fallibility. We are imperfect humans making judgements in an imperfect world. Judgements do need to be made, sin recognized and dealt with, victims cared for and truth told. The whole of Scripture tells of a grappling towards justice, however imperfect, a grappling that involves challenge, bitter argument, proactive listening to unheard voices, and a ready suspicion against the perspectives of the powerful, because it is easy for the powerful to impose their own perspective and erase that of others. Yet all of this in Scripture also needs holding within a wider framework of self-awareness: the call narrative of many prophets starts with an admission of their own sin and need for transformation (Isaiah, Ezekiel), while their call for justice is interwoven with lament for the coming judgement. Working towards justice involves an awareness of our limitations, willingness to enter the perspective of the other, willingness to be changed ourselves and adapt and reassess our own understanding of justice – and willingness to make space for gracious change to be possible for others too.

When I teach about Jesus, I often start with an exercise designed to bring unconscious thoughts and preferences to the surface, a heart perspective, rather than a head perspective, and get students to explore how the words 'Jesus Christ' carry different meanings in the spirituality of different people and groups. I scatter paintings of Jesus all over the room, from many different cultures, times, stories. Some try to be historical, but most represent how different cultures understand Christ within the concepts and imaginations of their own contexts. Then I ask group members to pick which image represents Jesus most closely for them, and which is furthest from who they think Jesus is. Most of the time, there is quite a wide spread. One year, however, the results astonished me. The group I was working with was a wonderfully mixed community from all over the world, from different denominations, cultures, countries and languages. Yet they divided into two very clear 'camps'. One held all the white participants from Global North countries, and all of them had chosen a picture of an embrace, of Jesus holding another person, and they spoke of love, acceptance and inclusion, of Jesus not turning people away, not being harsh and condemning. Their least favourite were a cluster of pictures including Jesus' anger when clearing the Temple, and images of drastic pain in the crucifixion. The other half of the group, all from the Global South, many from war-torn countries, picked pictures of Jesus on the cross as their favourite, and spoke of justice and the ravages of sin and the need for Jesus to come to make things right, starting with them. This kind of radical split has never occurred in any other group I have worked with, however diverse. But it was fascinating that to those living largely in comfort and plenty, acceptance and inclusion of the self was all-important, while for those who lived in difficult circumstances, justice and sin loomed large. In the second group, talk of love, inclusion and acceptance was meaningless unless accompanied by justice. They are two sides of the same coin. How important justice is, and what shape justice takes, is deeply rooted in context and life experiences.

Questions for reflection

1 What would 'contagious holiness' look like in the bitter world of current public debates, particularly online?
2 What are your favourite stories or sayings of Jesus? Why?
3 Which do you find difficult? Why do you think that is?

Pursuing justice in the refugee camps of Lebanon

One of the most moving stories I have heard of embracing the other in search of justice comes from the refugee camps of Lebanon, where millions of Syrians have fled violence. Lebanon hosts more refugees per capita than any other country in the world apart from Aruba (over a hundred times more than the UK). The vast majority of the refugees are Muslim, a mixed multitude in terms of background, socio-economics, political affiliation and the role they played or not in the conflict. A disproportionate number are families with children or older persons. Those who are able-bodied and have access to money have more ability to seek asylum elsewhere, to try and travel to wealthier countries.

Izdihar Kassis, a Christian leader living in Lebanon for many years, is the founder of a charity, Together for the Family, which started with offering trauma counselling for children and teenagers but has now expanded to a wide range of services including help with basic necessities, training for employment and medical care. Here she talks to me about her work.

IH: Tell me about an aspect of the work that is really precious to you.

IK: We host a monthly meeting for teenage girls. Many are in tough situations and have to go to work, whereas the boys go to school. Girls are expected to marry around 13 or 14. One girl used to come to our monthly meeting. She burnt herself to death. Her friend took a video of her in the bath then blackmailed her for money. She threatened to show the video to men. This young girl was so pretty, so beautiful. She lived in a tent, her father worked in the fields, and they saved money in a plastic pot. She took all the money. Her father discovered it. Her parents beat her really badly. They destroyed her body, burnt her with a hot knife and cigarettes so no man would ever look at her, so she would be ugly. She had no parents, no friends, no community left. I wasn't there when it happened. When I came home from travelling, she was dead. Her mum became crazy, and her dad escaped to Syria. It's a pretty typical story in the camps here.

Our ministry is to support these girls, support their self-esteem, strengthen their confidence to say no. We do a Bible study, tell them about God's love for them, how unique they are, how Jesus looks at them. We provide one-to-one counselling, and we discuss their stories all together.

I will tell you another case, very different. This girl, she was treated badly by her parents, told she was a burden on them. She had no motivation to live. We brought her to sewing school, taught her, gave her a sewing machine, encouraged her to start a business. Her father refused, because he doesn't want her to see anyone else. She self-harms, cuts her hands. So I asked her, 'What can we do for you?' She said, 'I need work. I need money for myself. I can't be a girl, buy things for myself like girls do.' I offered her a job, and said I will talk to your parents. You can work as an assistant to our sewing teacher. You will be protected there, we will look after you. Her parents agreed, because I am the only one who can give her a job, because we are safe.

After a month, things got bad again. Her parents took all her money, for food and basic necessities. I had a meeting with the mother. I told her, if you take all the money, she can't work any more. She needs to be able to nurture her self-esteem. Finally, her parents agreed, and now she is fine. She wants to be in our centre all the time. She's very open to me about all her relationships. Now she can love. It took three years, but now we see fruit. She's 17.

As Syrian girls, they feel that they are treated like animals. There's a lot of racism against the refugees here. We work to help them get over this, and meet together as Syrians, 120 girls altogether. They build relationships, give mutual support, and we offer advocacy and counselling.

IH: What are the challenges of your work, and what keeps you going?

IK: It's a very large community, there are huge needs. Sometimes I feel that's enough, I am tired of hearing these stories, I am traumatized myself from doing this.

Our charity now has 26 people working here in Lebanon, and 26 in Syria, all trained in trauma counselling. We have many different programmes: support for families with newborn babies, women refugees support group, teen girls support group, trauma work with women and with youth, trauma training for Syrian church leaders, vocational training for young women, preschool for rejected and/or disabled children (who are not accepted into the main schools for refugees), basketball and soccer for youth, boys' club, medical and dental care, food distribution, carpentry school, sewing school, traditional baking school and farming training.

Now in Lebanon there is a big economic crisis. Sixty per cent of Lebanese live under average income. Lots of refugees lost their jobs as a result. There's a lot of anger, a lot of stealing in the camps. We have 2.5 million refugees in Lebanon. Some of them are not easy to deal with, they are different. You never know whether they might be ISIS, have weapons in their tents and will threaten you. So we try to rescue the children, the babies, the women. Often I'm scared, I don't know what I will find when I enter a tent. It is not a normal place. You should expect problems every minute. These people are hurt and broken, and nobody cares about them. So we have to do it and tell them that God loves them.

Together for the Family (TFF) work for justice on a broad canvas. The vision that animates their work is deeply Christian, and hangs on a simple idea, to 'transform society through the next generation'. They started with children, because they recognized that the only way to stop an endless cycle of violence and revenge is to help children grow up with a different imagination. And to do this, trauma counselling was needed as a very first step. Healing the person so that they can engage positively with the world around them, know they are loved and learn to love others, is key to the vision. To do justice in these camps is to start with love and acceptance, regardless of how difficult this might be. As their work widened, TFF began to offer practical love and hope to more refugees, though they concentrate on those who, within the wider context of a disregarded, sometimes demonized group, are most invisible and unheard: the children and the women. To do justice means keeping an eye on both present and future, by meeting urgent needs, yet working with refugees to enable them to be full members of whichever society they settle into eventually, with skills and training as well as strengthened community bonds.

Questions for reflection

1 What would standing in solidarity with the churches in Lebanon look like?
2 Could you, your church, home group, commit to pray regularly for a group of Christians who may feel forgotten and abandoned?
3 How can you find out who is invisible or unheard in your local community?

Humanizing the other

How far should we take the metaphor of the embrace of the other in seeking justice? In the three stories in this chapter – Darren's, Jairus and the unnamed woman's, and Izdihar's, the person(s) doing the embracing are not ones who were hurt by the person being embraced. The Good Samaritan is more challenging, since the overwhelming prejudice of Israel against the Samaritans was harmful. It is much easier to offer an embrace when we are ourselves somewhat removed from a situation. It is easier to offer an embrace to those who are hurting and wronged, than to those who have caused the hurt. The metaphor of embrace however is primarily about a posture we choose to adopt, about having the willingness to meet the real and full person before us, and, before passing judgement, trying to see their story through their eyes, rather than tell *our* version of *their* story. Yet what if what was done amounts to terrible, unspeakable evil?

There is a feature of biblical talk about justice that often goes unnoticed. It is primarily communities and nations that are called to do justice. Individuals within them each have a responsibility, and a situation of personal sin by one person against another does require personalized responses. However, it is communities that are addressed again and again and exhorted to do good, to live well, to seek justice. The parable of the sheep and the goats (Matthew 25.31–40) is a case in point: it is mostly remembered for its stark imagery dividing people into two categories. The righteous/just will inherit the kingdom, and they are defined through their attitude to the hungry, thirsty, alien, naked, sick and prisoners. Readers and preachers often apply the parable's meaning to individuals and encourage personal righteousness and justice. While this is not wrong, it does miss the opening detail that people are being judged as groups. How does this help in looking at the metaphor of embrace?

As people are judged as 'nations', these will inevitably include a whole range of human beings, some with power, some without, oppressors and oppressed. To do justice is a communal vocation; it does not place the burden of meeting the other on one person only, let alone the person who was a victim. Rather, it calls the entire community to account for how they have conducted themselves in response to all, in many different configurations of justice and injustice, of power and complex relationships. Once again, the biblical text suggests that interconnected responsibilities towards one another come first, before individual rights. A communal approach ensures that undue burden is not placed on fragile or broken individuals; it also means that it becomes possible to love those who have failed before they are ready to make amends, or reach out to those they have hurt. The priority of love and embrace then makes it much easier for the offender to come to a place of considering their own actions.

For a community to embrace justice does not mean it forgoes judgement. Rather, it humanizes all involved in a given situation. Humanizing victims means not treating or seeing them simply as victims to be helped, but standing with them, working with them towards justice, witnessing to their suffering. It means seeing them in their fullness, as human beings whose stories are precious, yet not perfect, and whose entire life, in its triumphs and failures, its glimpses of holiness and moments of sin, needs to be part of moving forward. Equally, humanizing offenders/oppressors means not reducing them to the worst thing they have ever done, but seeing the brokenness and hurt within them too, while holding them responsible for their actions. To treat offenders as victims of circumstances without agency of their own, or to excuse their choices, would be to deny their essential humanity. To hold them accountable is to attend to their full humanity and free will, as moral persons with a conscience. Humanizing all involved in a situation enables complexity to be recognized, and hidden connections and links to deeper issues to emerge. Thinking back to Darren, once his full story is heard, uncomfortable questions arise about the community he grew up in, the different institutions he was in contact with, and the wider national scene of an extraordinarily wealthy country within which such stories are nevertheless all too common.

The process of 'humanizing' applies across all aspects of justice, whether judicial, interpersonal, societal or international. At every level, judgements need to be made, for the health of communities, and to act on the recognition of all victims of injustice as fully human, seen and heard by God. Yet at every level, to 'do justice' will probably be more complex and tortuous than expected, and attending to different narratives and perspectives makes judgement more difficult. It is easier to write off someone else, or an entire group, when we do not enter their stories. Stepping into their reality, even when we deeply disagree with them and their version of reality, forces us to consider how true and lasting justice can be done: unless the other is obliterated, lasting justice can only take root in partnership with those we have to keep living with, even if at a distance. A willingness to embrace means that we seek justice not simply for ourselves but also for the other: you do not have to agree with someone to seek justice on their behalf, and you do not have to forgo justice, compensation or reparations, to treat someone fairly and as made in the image of God.

Human beings find this task impossibly difficult. Archbishop Justin Welby, who has worked in international reconciliation in places of conflict for many years, often comments that the hardest thing in bringing together warring sides to explore justice and peace is for one side to tell the story of the other from their perspective. Instinctively, we cling to our own perspective, because to enter the perspective of the other inevitably changes our construction of the story, and the shape of our claim on the other. It allows us to start to understand the other's fear, trauma and experiences that have shaped their journey. It does not necessarily change fundamental appreciation of the rights and wrongs done, but it inevitably challenges both sides to consider a common narrative, which can never be identical to one side's only without creating new injustices.

Two sides of a dispute – those involved at the time – will rarely agree on what 'justice' looks like, if ever at all (just think of a quarrel between children and their competing claims). The matter becomes even more complex when we think of historical wrongs that still shape lives today. Waiting for full agreement to pursue justice is both impractical and unjust in itself, particularly when gross disparities in power, wealth and status foster ongoing injustice. It also fails to account for the reality of sin and human brokenness, which underlie, on the one hand, unwillingness to accept one's own wrongdoing, to let go of power, privilege and wealth, however unfairly gained, and on the other, desire for revenge, retribution and the obliteration of the other, or the ongoing effect of trauma and the need to make the future safe beyond what is possible. Judgements therefore have to be made before agreement can be reached, in the best way possible, bringing together as much understanding, openness and firmness in dealing with sin as can be, with an awareness that they may need revisiting in time. Therefore doing justice is not the task of today, but a path we set out on, that will constantly take us to new places. As Miroslav Volf points out, 'the human ability to agree on justice will never catch up with the human propensity to do injustice' (1996, p. 217).

The imperfection of human attempts to do justice inevitably points to mercy and forgiveness as an essential part of the process. Full justice is impossible this side of heaven, because even reparations and new ways of social organization can never erase the weight of the past, the ongoing effects of trauma, and new injustices arising. Therefore even when judgement is rendered, when wrongs have been righted as much as can be, something remains, and that something can only be dealt with through forgiveness. Forgiveness in this sense is writing off the possibility of a better past for the sake of a better future. It does not deny justice, it is integral to it, and fundamental in moving towards a better world.

Questions for reflection

1 Think of someone whom you profoundly disagree with.
2 Could you ask them to tell you their story, uninterrupted, and find another person to retell that story to, without inserting any of your own judgements within it?
3 How does this experience feel?

Prayer

Spend some time in silence, bringing to mind the faces of those you know who need justice, the faces of those you don't know but have seen on the news, and asking God to show you who else to pray for.

Try to dwell within this place, in the silence, without moving to solutions, but seeking to stand in solidarity and openness.

Then you may choose to pray the prayer below, from the Church of England, bringing each person to mind as you do so:

Living God,
deliver us from a world without justice
and a future without mercy;
in your mercy, establish justice,
and in your justice, remember the mercy
revealed to us in Jesus Christ our Lord.
Amen.[3]

---

3   See <www.churchofengland.org/prayer-and-worship/topical-prayers/prayers-world>.

5

Justice in the shape of a cross

All the themes and stories we have explored so far paint a rich and complex picture of justice, one where God consistently surprises his people in how he engages with them. The quest for justice and the fight against injustice underlie the whole story of God and his people, and the story is driven by love and relationship, neither of which can be divorced from justice questions. To love is to seek the best for the other; in a world where sin manifests itself through broken relationships that lead to exploitation, inequality and competition for resources and power, to speak of love will be to seek to restore relationships to their right balance. That restoration necessitates a vision for justice, for the right ordering of relationships between humanity, the earth and God. The Bible does not speak of love in disembodied ways, but in its real, practical outworkings. It is fundamentally incarnational, and therefore it is little surprise that all the themes explored so far find themselves united within one story, that of the life, death and resurrection of Jesus Christ. Jesus is the embodiment of God's justice and God's way of doing justice, as well as God's love for all humanity. Unsurprisingly, this embodiment is full of challenges for human beings who often prefer to pursue justice their own way. This chapter will concentrate on this story; there will be no stories from outside, simply a journey through the life, death and resurrection of Christ.

Justice in the ministry of Jesus

'To bring good news'
Key text: Luke 4.16–29

In Luke's Gospel, Jesus is baptized and led to the desert to be tempted, and on his return, filled with the Spirit, he teaches and preaches, including here, in Nazareth, his home town. Yet things take a difficult turn. Why would this be? His opening words in the synagogue quote Isaiah, and wonderful promises of justice and freedom. Right at the beginning, the good news Jesus proclaims is good news for the whole person – to the poor, the captive, the blind and the oppressed. It is tempting to spiritualize his words, and take them as metaphors for captivity to sin, or spiritual oppression. Yet everything in the Old Testament (Jesus' Scriptures) says otherwise. Jesus' future ministry also says otherwise, as he consistently attends to bodies – broken bodies, hurting bodies, hungry bodies, rejected bodies. Physical pain and oppression are a symptom of sin, and there is no divide here between body and spirit, between the spiritual and the secular. Poverty is as much a spiritual problem as a material one. So are unequal wealth and privilege. Jesus' proclamation was good news to many, and threatening to others. The crowds, initially, are enthusiastic and inspired – until Jesus offers a commentary on prophetic ministry.

Jesus goes to prophets Elijah and Elisha and their works, rather than words. The words prophets left behind can be twisted. Records of their actions speak loudly. Jesus highlights an uncomfortable discrepancy. The words of prophets were often words of challenge to Israel itself, to call it to repent and seek justice, mercy and true worship. The works of Elijah and Elisha mentioned here ministered not to Israel but to Gentiles, Naaman the Syrian, and the widow of Zarephath. Jesus' words are incendiary! Palestine in the first century was occupied territory, conquered and controlled by the Roman Empire, often in brutal and tyrannical ways. Hearing the prophecy of Isaiah, listeners would have assumed that they, themselves, were the poor, the oppressed, the prisoners, and that Jesus was proclaiming an end to Roman oppression. Good news. They may also have implicitly looked forward to the next line of the prophecy, which Jesus misses out, promising judgement on the Day of the Lord – judgement they would have expected to befall their enemies, the Romans.

Jesus' words reverse their expectations and suggest that God extends mercy to Gentiles, and that often, as with the prophets, the people of God fail to embody their vocation to be a light to the nations, through justice in their own communities and in their dealings with all. Jesus does not offer cheap salvation, and does not collude with the idea that the problem is always, or only, other people. He refuses an imagination that casts one nation as fully righteous and another as fully corrupt, which dehumanizes all involved. Jesus challenges the idea that they are the privileged recipients of divine love, regardless of their own actions. They were chosen and loved, but so are all other people on earth; their election was for the sake of the nations, to be a blessing to others, not to hoard power and status. We often react this way to talk of justice, arguing the other is unjust and deserves judgement, while we are victims and innocent and deserve kindness and grace. Jesus instead challenges listeners to recognize their own need for trans- formation, before trying to change the other. He does not condone Roman oppression, but refuses to enter a logic of revenge, violence and denial of the other's humanity.

The links between this passage and the preceding one, the testing of Jesus in the desert, are striking. In the wilderness, the devil shows Jesus 'all the kingdoms of the earth' (Luke 4.5) and offers them to him. Why would this be a 'temptation'? Jesus, as God, already had all the power anyone could possibly want; he could have bent human wills to his in an instant. In an instant, poverty and oppres- sion could have disappeared, together with inequality, hunger and pain. The temptation is to overpower the whole of humanity 'for the greater good', to pursue the right end through the wrong means.

But the whole point of the Incarnation is for the one who is all- powerful to enter the life of his creation – limited, vulnerable, and often powerless even when it thinks itself powerful. The Incarnation disrupts an imagination of justice that rests on power and external intervention, and proclaims a different way: compassion, identification and partnership. Power is tempting because it is a shortcut, and much less costly for the one who wields it. For power to come in humility and openness to the other takes a complete shift of one's position: inverting the self in order to understand the other and seek solutions that affirm and respect their humanity. The Incarnation is the ultimate proclamation of the worth and dignity of human beings. Jesus resists the temptation of power, because it would dehumanize the people he seeks to rescue, remove their free will, and bypass relationship.

In the synagogue, Jesus embodies the choice he made in the desert – to work towards salvation from within, accepting the risk and vulnerability it entails. When the people are enraged by his words, they threaten to throw him off the cliff – an echo of the third temptation, when the devil dares Jesus to throw himself off a cliff, so that, if he is the Son of God, God's angels would 'bear him up'. Jesus withstood that temptation, and was not given practical proof that he would be rescued. Here in Nazareth, he has to face the reality of vulnerability and injustice at the hands of other human beings, with no assurance of invulnerability. God's way of bringing about justice seems rather different from what humanity had imagined – or prayed for.

Breaking down barriers

This opening salvo introduces another central thread connected to justice – crossing and removing boundaries that have turned into barriers and justifications for unfairness, exploitation and marginalization. Boundaries and barriers are not the same thing. Boundaries mark out identity and difference, they create safe spaces within which to belong and explore identity as individuals and communities. Boundaries can be crossed, or moved, but their presence marks the crossing or movement as something significant – whether desirable or not. Boundaries make talk of identity possible. Crossing boundaries is essential to meet with the 'other':

if I want to truly listen, I have to move out of my 'comfort zone' and journey towards somebody else's, without trying to invade or reshape that other person's inner space, or letting go of my own sense of identity.

Boundaries can, however, solidify into barriers that prevent meeting others, keep them out and intensify invisibility and disconnection. Barriers are often erected out of fear – to protect from another deemed dangerous or abusive, to prevent contamination, to preserve privilege, to ward off change and transformation, to avoid the claims that the other might have on us. Barriers feel safer, but they are restrictive, and prevent us from seeing those outside our restricted field of vision. Boundaries and barriers matter in talk of justice, because they form part of how individuals, communities and societies shape their life, define what is 'good' and justify certain arrangements, even if they are unjust or damaging.

Boundaries and barriers abound in all places and times. Within the context of Jesus' ministry, there were sharp boundaries between Jew and Gentile, between Roman citizens and others, free and slave, man and woman. Many of those boundaries had solidified into barriers, the type of barrier that prevented many Jews from seeing a Samaritan as 'neighbour', or caused horror at the thought of Jesus widening the circle of 'good news' beyond Israel. The boundaries of the law had meant to enable Israel to create a distinctive community centred on God, held up by the covenant, as an example of a just and righteous way of living, so that others would be blessed. Often, the boundaries marked out the expression of justice, of care for the vulnerable, or the circumscribing of power so that leaders would not overreach. Yet turned into barriers, these boundaries had become a separating wall, preventing reaching out and blessing, and erecting walls within Israel itself. Those with disabilities were kept away from the Temple; the poor and destitute seen with suspicion; those labelled 'sinners' shunned and excluded. All these boundaries had been porous throughout the history of Scripture, with stories of Gentiles worshipping God and working with God, such as Melchizedek (meaning King of Justice/Righteousness) in Genesis 14, a 'priest of the Most High', who comes from outside the story and the line of revelation to Abraham; Pharaoh's daughter; Moses' father-in-law Jethro, who advises Moses on leading the people; the prostitute Rahab, who becomes part of Israel (Joshua 2; 6); Jael the Kenite (Judges 4—5), celebrated for her role in delivering Israel; Ruth the Moabite, who becomes part of Israel and, like Rahab, ancestor to David and Jesus.

Yet the ministry of Jesus shows, again and again, that boundaries had solidified and crossing them was frowned upon. Jesus' willingness to eat with outcasts, to feast with 'sinners', to heal across ethnic lines, to talk to women directly, challenged the identity of those around him. Jesus crossing the barriers proclaims that compassion and mercy are primary, that 'good news' is on offer to all, and perceived social worth is irrelevant. Jesus' actions shake the foundations of a social order that ensured stability in social status and hierarchy. They also challenge the sharp distinctions drawn by those with the power to put up barriers: again and again, Jesus challenges their perception of their own righteousness and worth, as in Luke 18.9–14:

> He also told this parable to some who trusted in themselves that they were righteous and regarded others with contempt: 'Two men went up to the temple to pray, one a Pharisee and the other a tax-collector. The Pharisee, standing by himself, was praying thus, "God, I thank you that I am not like other people: thieves, rogues, adulterers, or even like this tax-collector. I fast twice a week; I give a tenth of all my income." But the tax-collector, standing far off, would not even look up to heaven, but was beating his breast and saying, "God, be merciful to me, a sinner!" I tell you, this man went down to his home justified rather than the other; for all who exalt themselves will be humbled, but all who humble themselves will be exalted.'

Jesus here does not reverse the dichotomy of righteous vs sinner, but collapses it; he exposes how self-righteousness becomes a barrier to receiving grace and mercy. Both men are equally in need of, and equally offered, mercy. The boundary between right and wrong is not removed. Jesus still talks of sin and wrong, but talks about it within the context of grace, not a boundary to create divisions and hierarchies of worth, but a boundary to enable the flourishing of all. The Sermon on the Mount is striking in this respect; it is deeply ethically demanding, and uncompromising in its call for justice and righteousness, and, as such, levels the playing field by showing that all fall short and need grace. The good news is that this grace is freely available to those who recognize their need for it.

From scarcity to abundance

Free abundant grace disrupts the economy of scarcity that gives rise to barriers, injustice and anxiety. The whole ministry of Jesus is lived out under the sign of abundance. This is clearest in the Gospel of John, as the inauguration of Jesus' public ministry comes with turning water into wine at a wedding (John 2.1–11). The miracle symbolizes sharing in joy and celebration, and recalls the profusion of creation. Jesus does not just turn water into wine, it turns it into gallons and gallons of the absolutely best wine! It is a clear sign, right at the beginning, that something new is taking place, that the fierce competition for resources, status and wealth cannot have the final word. The proclamation of the abundance of God is a cornerstone in the proclamation of justice and new life, because it resets imaginations and expectations. Sadly, human beings have tried to change the wine back into water ever since.

The best-known story of abundance in the ministry of Jesus is the feeding of the five thousand in the key text Mark 6.30–44.

This story puts a heavy emphasis on human need: the disciples' need for refreshment and rest; the crowds' need for teaching and guidance, because they were 'like sheep without a shepherd', and everyone's need for food, at the end of a long day. Need is great to start with, and the disciples are overwhelmed. They encountered need on their travel, and need now. In an economy of scarcity, need can quickly become either overwhelming or something we get used to and stop noticing. Jesus, however, draws attention to need, and his immediate reaction is 'compassion'. Deep, existential need that remains unmet (because they are 'without a shepherd') necessitates a response, one that cares for the whole person; Jesus does not simply teach them with words, but anchors his teaching in action, caring for their bodies as well as their spiritual needs. Once again, the whole person is looked after, with seamless continuity between theoretical and practical message.

The disciples, however, struggle to understand. They cannot see how such a crowd can be fed. There is not enough food, not enough money. Despite having seen miracles already, despite hearing Jesus teach, their thinking is still rooted in an economy of scarcity that reduces Jesus to ordinary human proportions and expects everyone to look after themselves. The miracle anchors Jesus' words in experience and reality. Just as in Cana, the generosity of God far exceeds expectations. Not only is a crowd fed, but there are plenty of leftovers! The leftovers challenge the economy of scarcity. When our view of the world is constricted, shaped by fear of scarcity, the word of the day is efficiency and maximizing returns. Everything must be used, everyone must work as effectively as possible, and waste is not tolerated. The disciples' solution, for everyone to disperse and find food for themselves, may have seemed more efficient. But in the economy of the kingdom of God, things are different, and everyone has their fill – and more, to give away. The picture is reminiscent of the manna and quail in the desert, or the command to always leave enough for the poor to glean during a harvest. When use of resources and people is maximized, and waste is cut, the risk is that the most vulnerable are left without leftovers, forgotten and invisible if they themselves cannot contribute. In an economy of scarcity, there is no room for grace.

Often this story is read in isolation, standing on its own. Yet it belongs together with the passage that immediately precedes it: a very different banquet, held by Herod, which culminates with the demand for John the Baptist's head on a platter, in the key text Mark 6.17–29.

The two feasts could not be more different. One where everyone is invited, with no distinction of status or wealth. The other, behind closed doors, for the rich and privileged only. One with simple fare, the king and his disciples themselves serving the crowd. The other, a complex feast around an earthly king served by many servants. One, a celebration of life, the other, with a crowning death. Those two scenes contrast the two economies: Herod's economy of empire, based on brutality, repression and disregard for life, and the other, Jesus' economy of abundance, based on generosity, inclusion and compassion. It is the colliding of these two imaginations that causes increasing conflict throughout the ministry of Jesus, because empire and compassion are diametrically opposed, and Jesus' determination to break down barriers, to invite all closer to God, and place compassion first, threatens the very foundations of empire, not just for Herod, but also for all the little empires that human beings build for themselves, in families, in businesses, in religious settings. Empire and scarcity go together, because scarcity justifies the hoarding of resources, and ruthlessness in defending one's right to their share. The kind of generosity at the root of the laws of the Old Testament – providing for the poor and vulnerable even in times of personal challenge and scarcity – finds itself embodied in the actions of Jesus.

Questions for reflection

1 Where around you can you see signs of God's abundance? How could you celebrate these?
2 What boundaries are important to you? Are there any barriers? Why are they there?
3 Have you ever been kept out, or affected by someone else's boundaries and barriers? How did that feel? Why do you think those were there?

A radical reconfiguration of power

There are many parts of the life of Jesus we could examine, and the same themes would resonate: meeting people, seeing and helping others be seen, hearing and helping others listen and hear, caring and healing, while challenging sin and its impact. A collision course with the crowds and the powers of the day becomes inevitable as even crowds and disciples baulk at the radical transformation Jesus preaches. In the Gospel of John, the feeding of the five thousand occurs at the beginning of chapter 6, followed the next day by his teaching on the 'bread of life'. Miracle and teaching do not yield a compliant crowd, eager to follow, but a crowd full of questions, doubts and pushback. In 6.41, 'the Jews began to complain about him because he said, "I am the bread that came down from heaven."' In 6.60, 'When many of his disciples heard it, they said, "This teaching is difficult, who can accept it?"', and in 6.61, Jesus is aware that his disciples are complaining about him. In 6.66, 'Because of this many of his disciples turned back and no longer went about with him.' It is easy to imagine the ministry of Jesus as drawing in lots of crowds eagerly following while some powerful, self-righteous people stood against him – and, possibly, imagine ourselves as eager followers. This is not the picture we find in the Gospels, however. Everyone found Jesus difficult. There were friends, listeners and enemies in all strata of society, within and without Israel. Even his closest disciples and friends struggled to understand him, at times questioning his choices and teaching. Compassion does not build empires, it challenges them, and the challenge is painful. This increasing opposition highlights the difficulty of bringing about justice and good news, in continuity with the struggles of prophets like Jeremiah. In the ministry of Jesus, to bring good news is an ambiguous business, because 'good news' involves death to sin, and justice, embracing those we would rather not go near.

The controversy surrounding Jesus' ministry reflects his challenge to structures of power, at micro and macro levels, a challenge that comes primarily through the embrace he offers to all, irrespective of rank or supposed worthiness – social or moral. In Jesus, we see power divesting itself from all its usual outward signs, yet still, undeniably, powerful. There is a deep contradiction, almost, at the heart of the life and death of Jesus. He demonstrates power over nature in calming the storm and walking on water; power over illnesses of the body and the heart; power to forgive sins; power to change lives. And yet this power is entirely channelled through deep openness to the other, invitation rather than coercion, gentleness rather than harshness, grace rather than punishment. And this power is held within a frail, fragile human body: Jesus gets hungry, thirsty, tired, sad. His power is constantly directed towards the welfare and transformation of the people whose lives he has come to share, and he has compassion for the pain and oppression that they endure, and for their unwillingness to change – as we see in his cry over Jerusalem:

> As he came near and saw the city, he wept over it, saying, 'If you, even you, had only recognized on this day the things that make for peace! But now they are hidden from your eyes. Indeed, the days will come upon you, when your enemies will set up ramparts around you and surround you, and hem you in on every side. They will crush you to the ground, you and your children within you, and they will not leave within you one stone upon another; because you did not recognize the time of your visitation from God.'
> (Luke 19.41–44)

Jesus' words here echo the words of many Old Testament prophets, who simultaneously called for justice and judgement, and wept over the fate of those under judgement.

Jesus' reconfiguration of power comes into sharp relief in the account of the washing of the feet in the key text, John 13.1–16.

This passage is so well known that we may lose sight of its force and radical challenge. First, of course, is the image of Jesus taking on a menial role in the eyes of a hierarchical, honour-based society. As feet got dirty in the dust and dirt of a warm country, coming into a dwelling usually meant either washing one's feet or having them washed, normally by a servant or slave, or someone of lesser status (women, sometimes children). Very occasionally, a host might wash the feet of an honoured guest. But the person with most honour (a form of social power) would never wash others' feet. By washing the disciples' feet, Jesus does two important things. One, he affirms their immense human dignity and the image of God within them; second, he repudiates any form of social hierarchy and distinctions of status. The disciples are all 'loved to the end', and they are all treated as honoured and respected. Jesus does not, however, treat them as more honoured than him ('no greater than their master'), but invites them to imitate him. He is still 'Teacher and Lord', but his role does not lead him to treat others as lesser than him. His actions challenge the disciples in their relationships with one another, and the ways in which leadership and power are inhabited.

Perhaps a surprising element of the story is the emphasis on betrayal which bookends the first part of the narrative. Jesus 'loves his own', even though 'his own' includes Judas. There is no caveat, no sense that Judas is any less loved, or any less served. Judas has his feet washed, is treated with the same respect as other disciples. At one level, this heightens the drama of the scene. But at another, it challenges how sin, evil and failure are approached: after Jesus' death, I wonder how the disciples recalled the foot washing, which included Judas, and how this shaped their feelings and responses. The passage speaks truth and does not sugar-coat Judas' actions. He betrayed Jesus, and this betrayal is made all the worse by the love that Jesus displayed towards him. Yet at the same time, if Jesus treated him with love and respect regard-less, still a human being made in the image of God, shouldn't the disciples do the same, even at the height of despair or anger fol-lowing the crucifixion?

A pattern is set for the life of the community to come in how to treat offending members. All four Gospels state that Jesus knew one of the disciples would betray him. He was not naive, nor did he hide the reality of the coming betrayal. His allusions to betrayal gave Judas a chance to come clean, or turn away from the course he had set. Jesus had the power to stop Judas, to make him change – but did not use it. We can find many justifications – he knew that the cross was necessary, or what Judas was going to do would have been done by another. Yet alongside these is the fact that Jesus does not use his power to violate human free will and responsibility. Judas is invited to change, never forced. The radical equality and dignity embodied in the washing of feet applies to all – without exception. In Mark 14.21, Jesus alludes to the dire consequences of Judas' choice: 'For the Son of Man goes as it is written of him, but woe to that one by whom the Son of Man is betrayed! It would have been better for that one not to have been born.' There will be accountability and consequences (though these are not spelt out), yet, accountability does not negate Judas' humanity or dignity, and does not distort Jesus' relationship to him. Jesus' attitude to Judas embodies holding together love and justice.

There is one more aspect to the story that we often forget to comment on. Jesus is by far the most powerful person in the scene. He is by far the most powerful person in the whole of the Gospels – even though others might think they have power over him. The mess of the world around him is not his – he has not contributed to sin and brokenness, quite the opposite. Yet, in the Incarnation, Jesus shows that power cannot be a bystander: either it works towards liberation, or it colludes with the forces of oppression. In Jesus, God works for transformation and justice now. He does not wait for the oppressed to rise up, for the weak to stand up to the strong, as human beings so frequently do. (How often do we expect the one woman in a room to call out sexism? Or the one person with a disability to speak on disability questions?) Jesus shoulders the responsibility for change, and invites all to join in the work. Power is deeply reconfigured into responsibility towards the other; and, even more surprisingly for all those who watched the unfolding events, Jesus reconfigured power further – in the form of a cross, bearing himself the cost of the change he was bringing about.

Questions for reflection

1 What power do you think you hold? What power do others think you hold? What might you be called to do with the power or influence you do have?

2 What do you think you would have found difficult about Jesus, had you been present back then?

3 Compassion is a clear call of the gospel. Who do you have compassion for? Might God be calling you to extend that compassion further, perhaps in costly ways? Who might help you on that journey?

The cross as the unexpected embodiment of justice

The story of Jesus' crucifixion is redolent with allusions to justice, and the abuse of justice. It contrasts sharply the flawed workings of human 'justice' with the embodiment of the justice of God in Jesus.

The justice of the elders, Pilate and Herod
Key text: Luke 22.66—23.25

The story that starts in the garden with the arrest of Jesus is a familiar one. Someone who challenges the social order, privilege and inequality is labelled dangerous for the peace and stability of the nation. Jesus' ministry, based on compassion, crossed boundaries and affirmed the value of those who were disregarded. Compassion takes pain and oppression seriously, and affirms that they are neither normal nor inevitable. As such, the ministry of Jesus inevitably called for change at a wider level. Change means a degree of instability and struggle to find a 'new normal', which threatens current distributions of wealth and power. The story of the 'trial' of Jesus reprises a common motif of the Old Testament: it is easy for the powerful to twist the instruments of justice to serve their own ends, rather than the people they were intended to protect. The powerful can twist both the wider narrative of justice – who 'deserves' to be respected, privileged, comfortable (as opposed to 'tax collectors, sinners and prostitutes') – and the judicial system, the instrument used to remedy injustice.

Jesus had already appeared before 'the elders of the people', the chief priests and scribes, who performed a cursory interrogation, and set themselves as witnesses, judge and jury. Jesus cuts a lonely figure against the might of the elders. The charges they then bring to Pilate do not properly reflect their interrogation. They focus on the nation and taxes, to curry favour from the Romans (to bias the judge), and a claim that Jesus said he was the Messiah (he did not actually say so in response to their direct question, although it could be inferred from his answer). There is much irony in the claims about the nation and taxes, given the underlying hatred of Romans and longing for independence. The ministry of Jesus in Luke had started with his skirmish in the synagogue, precisely for being inclusive in his proclamation of the good news. Now he stands accused of hostility to Rome. The accusation uncovers the self-serving nature of these elders, whose allegiance sways with their own interest. Later, they 'vehemently accuse him' before Herod. The justice of the people of God, supposedly rooted in Torah, was to be distinctive, to avoid partiality, false accusations and biased judgement. It was justice meant to protect the widow, the orphan and the stranger, to limit revenge and let justice shape the imagination. Like many kings and rulers before them, the elders pervert the judicial system. Their portrayal is somehow less sympathetic than that of Pilate and Herod, who have doubts – though only because they do not have the same vested interest. In the end, Pilate and Herod 'become friends' as a result of the episode, even though they had been enemies. This aside highlights how injustice often enables bonding between those in power in their efforts to consolidate and preserve their status. To stay in power matters more than what had divided them, and joining forces allows them to develop a common narrative to justify their actions.

Human justice is shown as fragile, easily perverted and subject to the desires of sinful human beings. A retributive or remedial justice system cannot work well unless the wider imagination and social organization are themselves infused with justice for all. Meanwhile, human leaders fail to use their power appropriately. The elders use theirs to vilify and condemn an innocent man. Herod and Pilate fail to stand for truth and right, and cave in to the populist demands of an excited mob. Justice fails actively and passively, through what is done, and what fails to be done.

The justice of Herod, Pilate and the elders is also curiously disembodied, abstracted from relationships and connection to the wider community. None of them know Jesus personally, they report hearsay and accusations. There is no deep searching for truth, and Jesus himself refuses to play a game of cat and mouse with those who care neither for truth nor justice, but for their own interest and political survival. Hence he stays silent. There is no meeting of persons, no listening, no compassion. The elders ignore Jesus' popularity and the lives changed through his ministry. Pilate and Herod make decisions based on political expediency and the short-term gain of pleasing the crowd that happens to have gathered on the day. The idea of the common good is used instrumentally, to achieve secondary aims that have little to do with justice. Ultimately, Jesus is condemned despite Herod and Pilate both agreeing he does not deserve to die. Justice is meant to witness to truth and vision in the public square, to enable the righting of wrongs, and fair judgement that helps sustain peace and justice in the wider community, and shape its moral imagination. Here, truth does not matter, the public declaration of truth (Jesus does not deserve to die) is ignored, wrongs are enacted in the course of judicial proceedings, rather than resolved by them, and judgement reflects desires for revenge and the annihilation of someone who embodies challenge.

What kind of moral imagination might be shaped by such perversion of justice? Ultimately, this is the justice of empire and scarcity – justice in the service of oppressive power, dispensed by the powerful only, with the aim of preserving their way of life and justifications for it, the people simply tools to use or discard, rather than to know, care for and cherish. The crowds meanwhile participate in their leaders' decision by calling for unjust results. The latter part of the story mirrors the earlier: Jesus, like John the Baptist, is caught up in the economy of scarcity, in power plays between rulers, and, by his very being, threatens the powerful, who hasten to eliminate the threat. It is little surprise that their justice ends with a cross – a human invention with no purpose but torture and intimidation, a way to spread fear and reinforce the existing distribution of wealth and power.

The justice of the cross

Meanwhile, Jesus stands alone, his entire life speaking of a different kind of justice. Jesus had spent his life reaching out in love to the people that the leaders pretend to look out for, but shy away from. The narrative of the cross stands in continuity with Jesus' life: it speaks of the ongoing battle between two different ways of looking at the world, of the dangers of preaching justice and equality, and Jesus' solidarity with the people, even when many turn against him. We cannot understand God's justice in the cross unless we read it within the framework of the life and ministry of Jesus. All the meaning that is read into the cross retrospectively – salvation, atonement, substitution – is tied to the wider story of the proclamation of love and justice embodied and embedded within one, simple life.

The universal meaning of the cross is intimately tied to its particularity. It is in the life of Jesus, in his relationships, in his care and love for those around him, in his arguments on understanding the Law and the Prophets, in his offer of forgiveness to sinners and his challenge to those who thought themselves righteous, that an alternative to Herod's imagination and justice are found. Jesus does not save the world from a neutral, external position, but from within, in identifying with the heart of the human condition: its vulnerability, its limitations in time, space and culture, its bodily constraints, its powerlessness against systems that dehumanize and destroy. If Jesus had used his power to free himself from Herod, Pilate and the crowds, he would have broken his identification with human beings. By surrendering and refusing to fight, he enters the otherness of humanity – to the very end.

The entire story of Scripture so far has borne a call for justice, tasked humanity with a vocation to pursue it, and witnessed to the struggles that justice provokes, within and between human beings. Here, we see human justice fail completely, and choose to condemn the very incarnation of justice. And yet, within the story of failure, a narrative of transformation is hidden, one that proclaims that the justice of God sweeps away, transforms and redefines what human beings think justice is. If justice was just deserts, then Jesus would have walked free. If justice was just deserts, every human being would be condemned. Therefore, either justice is swept aside in the cross or justice is not primarily about 'just deserts', but needs to be rethought, and anchored in the very attributes of God that have come through the story of Scripture: compassion, love, grace, covenant relationship.

Two others also, who were criminals, were led away to be put to death with him. When they came to the place that is called The Skull, they crucified Jesus there with the criminals, one on his right and one on his left. Then Jesus said, 'Father, forgive them; for they do not know what they are doing.' And they cast lots to divide his clothing. And the people stood by, watching; but the leaders scoffed at him, saying, 'He saved others; let him save himself if he is the Messiah of God, his chosen one!' The soldiers also mocked him, coming up and offering him sour wine, and saying, 'If you are the King of the Jews, save yourself!' There was also an inscription over him, 'This is the King of the Jews.'

One of the criminals who were hanged there kept deriding him and saying, 'Are you not the Messiah? Save yourself and us!' But the other rebuked him, saying, 'Do you not fear God, since you are under the same sentence of condemnation? And we indeed have been condemned justly, for we are getting what we deserve for our deeds, but this man has done nothing wrong.' Then he said, 'Jesus, remember me when you come into your kingdom.' He replied, 'Truly I tell you, today you will be with me in Paradise.'
(Luke 23.32–43)

At the time of crucifixion, Jesus' identification with humanity takes a further step. He is placed with criminals, with those who, by their own admission, have hurt others and deserve their sentence. Jesus does not identify with humanity partially, but completely. There is no human being that is beyond the scope of Christ: he prays for forgiveness for those who have hurt him – leaders, soldiers, angry crowds, bystanders. This is not a crusade for justice that seeks to annihilate those considered oppressors, evil, unjust, but one that seeks to embrace them, and invite them into life. On the cross, the taunts directed at Jesus echo Satan in the desert – if you are the Messiah/King of the Jews/Son of God, save yourself. This taunt bookends the beginning and end of Jesus' ministry. The temptation to misuse power and achieve justice in all the wrong ways is ever-present – and resisted. The cross affirms that there is another way, a better way.

The redefinition of justice is clear in Jesus' exchange with the second criminal. The first criminal does not care about who deserves to die; he does not look upon the other two with compassion, or even a sense of shared suffering. He simply mocks. The second man refuses to be a bystander, and, rather than focusing on his own pain – which must have been considerable – he challenges untruth and unfairness. He does so on the basis of a just deserts view of justice, that both criminals 'are getting what [they] deserve for their deeds', but Jesus is innocent. He turns to Jesus and asks, not for justice, not even for forgiveness, but for the possibility of grace – and grace is freely given. He uses the Old Testament formula for crying out to God – 'Remember me!' God's 'remembering' is always tied to compassion, responding to the people's pain, and an unbreakable relationship between God and his people. It has little to do with worth or deserts. Grace does not remove the man's sentence: he will still die. And yet, Jesus extends grace: the man is not mocked, dismissed or written off for what he has done. Jesus' own pain does not blind him to the need of the other – even the undeserving other. God's compassion reaches far beyond 'just deserts' and affirms the humanity, the lovability, the worth of a man who had almost given up on himself.

On the cross, ultimately, Jesus takes upon himself all the twisted, distorted notions of justice that humans have, and enters their consequences. He embraces the grief and pain of the condemnation of human beings, of just deserts for their actions. To bring about justice, salvation and transformation, Jesus does not solely enter the path of a victim, but stands in solidarity and understanding with sinners, oppressors, robbers, criminals . . . The whole of humanity is embraced on the cross, and this embrace yields a radical challenge to seeking justice:

The crucifixion articulates God's odd freedom, his strange justice, and his peculiar power . . . Without the cross, prophetic imagination will likely be as strident and as destructive

as that which it criticizes. The cross is the assurance that effective prophetic criticism is done not by an outsider but always by one who must embrace the grief, enter into the death, and know the pain of the criticized one.
(Brueggemann, 2018, p. 99)

At the heart of the cross, what stands as a monument to human foolishness is turned into a witness to God's grace, and a challenge to rethink how we pursue justice and peace within human communities.

The foolishness of the cross

For the message about the cross is foolishness to those who are perishing, but to us who are being saved it is the power of God. For it is written,

'I will destroy the wisdom of the wise,
and the discernment of the discerning I will thwart.'

Where is the one who is wise? Where is the scribe? Where is the debater of this age? Has not God made foolish the wisdom of the world? For since, in the wisdom of God, the world did not know God through wisdom, God decided, through the foolishness of our proclamation, to save those who believe. For Jews demand signs and Greeks desire wisdom, but we proclaim Christ crucified, a stumbling-block to Jews and foolishness to Gentiles, but to those who are the called, both Jews and Greeks, Christ the power of God and the wisdom of God. For God's foolishness is wiser than human wisdom, and God's weakness is stronger than human strength.
(1 Corinthians 1.18–25)

Paul's words are stark and uncompromising: the cross makes no sense. At least, not to the way in which humans normally think. It is people who thought themselves righteous, who ended up condemning the most righteous man there ever was; people who thought they were pursuing God, who put God to death. The cross does not make sense within an economy of scarcity driven by fear, where wrongdoers have to be severely punished for deterrence and to protect the community, where those in power justify making sacrifices ('collateral damage') for the common good. The cross is foolish, because grace does not make sense. Grace is patently unjust, completely underserved, it does not try to guarantee the future, it is freely offered with no ties, and cannot be imposed. Yet if God loves justice, and God's most complete revelation of himself in Jesus focuses on grace, then justice and grace, justice and mercy must belong together.

Grace goes against our deepest human instincts: the instinct to protect ourselves and those we love; the instinct to say, 'But they did...' and reach for retribution. The law of the talion – an eye for an eye – had instigated a limitation of revenge and retribution and established proportionality. In Jesus, the logic of escalating revenge is not merely restrained, but reversed into a prescription of escalating forgiveness, as Jesus tells his disciples to forgive seventy times seven times. Grace transforms the justice of scarcity, anxiety and fear, which only considers what one deserves or is entitled to, and moves into the realm of generosity, gift and hope.

How then do we reconfigure justice so that it walks hand in hand with mercy? The life of Jesus and the Old Testament have already given us the answer: by seeing, hearing and responding to the other, and choosing to humanize every person, by rooting justice in compassion, and an attempt to see the whole person, rather than reduce them to what they have or have not done. When grace and justice meet, the past is acknowledged and its consequences accepted, yet the future is not defined, reduced or diminished by this. Grace means that individuals and communities are no longer doomed to live for ever tied to the pain and consequences of past actions, but have a chance for transformation. Grace gives birth to hope, and hope strengthens our courage to work for a better future.

It is easy for the image of the cross and the concept of grace to be abused. Throughout history, the powerful have often told those they oppressed that their Christian duty was to forgive, or to be meek and willing to turn the other cheek. This was the case in church services on plantations that dehumanized, maimed and exploited slaves of African descent; it is the message many women hear in patriarchal contexts, that they should submit and humble themselves as Christ did; it is the twisted message often given to survivors of abuse, that they should forgive, forget and move on. But these examples profoundly distort the symbolism of the cross.

First, grace does not mean that there are no consequences to wrongdoing – rather, those consequences are not the end of the road, do not prevent God's presence, and, above all, do not mean that someone is less than human, unlovable, disposable. Second, to divorce grace from the pursuit of justice and the vision of community expressed in creation is to ignore the whole of the life of Christ: the cross and grace do not stand apart from everything else, but form a whole picture with Jesus' challenges to the sins, inequalities, injustices and oppressions of his day. It is precisely because these exist that grace is needed, grace that takes seriously the hurt and pain of sin and witnesses to it, grace that recognizes that all human beings are caught up in a web of relationships and systems that affect their ability to behave justly, and gives them a template for change. To misuse grace is to completely miss the radical reconfiguration of power in Jesus: that Jesus is the most powerful person within any encounter – but chooses to use power differently. To misuse grace to justify ongoing abuses of power, or to deny the reality and depth of sin and its impact, is to misuse power in precisely all the ways that Jesus challenged. Grace is indissolubly linked to compassion, to seeing the face of the other, hearing their voice, and accepting their claim on us. Compassion inherently precludes the misuse of power.

For justice to walk hand in hand with mercy, therefore, there needs to be an acknowledgement of truth – in all its ugliness and discomfort, including an acknowledgement that human imagination and reason are too small, too limited, to truly do justice. God's justice happens on a broader canvas, a cosmic, historical, universal canvas that sees and hears every cry, every heart, understands every influence, resistance and complicity. In other words, God's justice is far beyond our own. To do justice therefore, as human beings, means to join with what God himself is doing – and learn through the process, just as Moses did, that justice begins with a profound transformation of our imagination, desires and ways of being in the world. Justice is something to cultivate within ourselves and within our communities. It is not about merely knowing what is right, but about the kind of person we become. It is about being disciples of Jesus, committed to cultivating an attitude of openness and embrace towards those who surround us, so that we come to see the world through God's eyes, with the same eagerness for its healing and wholeness. Justice, in other words, is a vocation.

Questions for reflection

1 When have you experienced grace for yourself? How easy do you find it to accept grace – from God, from others, from yourself?
2 How do you feel about forgiveness and grace?
3 Can you think of a situation where you or someone you know might be called to hold together justice and grace? How might you go about it?

Justice, resurrection and ascension

The intertwining of justice, love and mercy stretches through the life and death of Jesus, all the way into his resurrection appearances. One of these, in the key text John 21.4–19, recounts Jesus' first proper resurrection meeting with Peter as he comes home from a night of unsuccessful fishing with other disciples.

Jesus had appeared a number of times already and, true to the pattern of his life, disrupted social expectations by appearing to women, who became the first witnesses to the resurrection. Peter and 'the disciple Jesus loved' had run to the tomb but found it empty, and did not know what to make of this. Despite several subsequent appearances, the men do not recognize Jesus as he appears after a night when they have fished in vain. The episode is reminiscent of another one involving Peter, unsuccessful fishing and a miraculous catch, this time at the beginning of the Gospel of Luke (5.1–11). There, Peter doubts Jesus' instructions, later recognizes him as somehow special, and follows him. Here, at the other end of the story, in John, there are no protestations. Despite not recognizing Jesus, the disciples let down their nets after their hard and empty night. In both stories, abundance shines through, as they catch an enormous amount of fish, with comparatively little effort. The reversal of scarcity and the return of the promise of abundance in creation continues beyond Jesus' earthly life. As a sign at the end of John's Gospel, it points to the trajectory of the work of Christ going forward, a continued encouragement for imagination and expectations to be reshaped. The whole of creation is being renewed. The disciple that Jesus loved recognizes him, but it is Peter who acts, rashly, as always. Peter does not need to see, or touch, or even hear Jesus himself. He simply 'heard that it was the Lord', and that was enough.

Jesus' last words to Peter had been a rebuke, as Peter tried to defend him and cut off a servant's ear (John 18.11). Despite years following Jesus, Peter still sought to fight for justice with a sword, exercising power over another. He was not singled out in any previous appearances. I wonder if he wondered why? He had been close to Jesus, closer than Thomas, for instance, who gets a special mention. Meeting in a crowd may have been awkward. Jesus had predicted that Peter would deny knowing him, three times, in the other Gospels. John only recounts Peter's denial – fear and self-preservation coming before his allegiance to Jesus. Peter had turned from participant to bystander when speaking up for justice and truth became too costly. What would a just response from Jesus to Peter be?

Peter's reaction is extreme, and a little comical. He was naked in the boat, a normal practice for fishermen, and, very logically, puts on clothes before jumping in to get to Jesus faster! The detail isn't there just for comic relief. Nakedness echoes the story of the garden of Eden, of Adam and Eve realizing they were naked, and covering themselves. As innocence is lost, human beings try to cover up their guilt and hide from God. Peter cannot bear to be just himself before Jesus. He covers up. But his guilt lies shallow before the surface. As they all get to the beach, they see that Jesus is cooking on a charcoal fire. This word for a charcoal fire is only used one other time – in John 18.18, as people warm themselves while Jesus is being tried, and Peter denies knowing Jesus. The gathering is very different this time, but the shadow of the first cannot be dispelled unless it is named, and dealt with.

Jesus' cooking meanwhile is a reminder of abundance and the feeding of the five thousand. Even the resurrected Christ cares about the disciples' bodies, exhausted and hungry after a night of fishing. The promise of abundance, of the hungry being fed, of true justice, is an integral part of the coming of the kingdom of God. John reminds us that it is the third time that Jesus has appeared to them. Peter denied Jesus three times, and it takes three appearances for him to start addressing the guilt eating at him. Most of the other disciples had fled too, back then. It is mostly women mentioned at the foot of the cross, staying with Jesus, in the strange solidarity of the disenfranchised and marginalized. It is those with little to lose who remain to the end, those for whom Jesus had meant liberation and justice to a greater degree. Did everyone know that Peter had disowned Jesus? The story does not tell. But Peter knows that Jesus knows, and that is what matters.

Jesus asks Peter, three times, 'Do you love me?' For someone who had been disowned, before being brutally killed while his friends fled, asking the question only three times seems very restrained! Peter does not simply answer 'yes', but insists, twice, 'you know that I love you'. Peter affirms his loyalty without referring to his failure; he wants to jump over the 'justice' part and move straight to grace, move to resurrection without going through the cross, rely on Jesus' knowledge of his heart to avoid naming the truth. But this will not do. Grace that bypasses truth and transformation is not true grace, because it bypasses justice. It is, in the famous words of Dietrich Bonhoeffer, 'cheap grace': 'the preaching of forgiveness without requiring repentance, baptism without church discipline, Communion without confession, absolution without personal confession. Cheap grace is grace without discipleship, grace without the Cross, grace without Jesus Christ, living and incarnate' (2015, p. 3). Here we come again to the indissoluble link between mercy and justice, and the fact that one cannot exist without the other. It would not honour Peter not to hold him accountable for his actions, nor would it enable him to grow into the man Jesus calls him to be, one who will 'feed his sheep'.

Finally, Peter acknowledges, 'Lord, you know everything.' This 'everything' is weighty, and Peter's upset shows that he recognizes the implicit message in the three questions. Jesus refers to it no more. It was not Jesus who needed to 'know', it was Peter – know that Jesus knew, and that grace was on offer. The three questions would have reminded the disciples of the prediction of threefold denial, and Jesus' address to Peter implicitly affirms his reinstatement, and the love that Jesus has for him. The episode is about the restoration of Peter, the mending and knitting together of the image of God within him, the repairing of the relationships between Peter and Jesus/God, Peter and the disciples, and Peter with himself. Based on the acknowledgement of the truth of who he is – sinful, yet forgiven and deeply loved – Peter is ready to receive a new vocation, to care for the people of Jesus. The past does not prevent his being trusted for the future, but the past acknowledged in truth shapes a different future, and Peter as a different leader, who knows his fallibility, knows the power of grace and the need to extend it to others. This commission, at the end of John, is one of care and nurture, to 'feed' and 'tend': the earthiness of the metaphor again ties together care of body and soul, and points to the need for justice and salvation for the whole person. It also reminds the disciples that care for other human beings, and for the community of faith, is valuable in and of itself; it is not instrumentalized, and does not need justifying. In an economy of scarcity, 'care' is rationed, often seen as time-consuming, costly or a hindrance to productivity and efficiency, or, at times, in the Church, mission or growth. In the economy of God's kingdom, to care is foundational, because human beings are made in the image of God. An ethic of care for its own sake is a central component in doing justice and practising mercy.

The account finishes with the troubling image of Peter's foreshadowed death. The man who had tried to defend Jesus with a sword, who had refused to risk death with Jesus and denied him, will be transformed beyond all expectations into a man who follows in the footsteps of Christ: refusing to misuse power, and choosing to proclaim a gospel of justice and mercy, of love and liberation, to the cost of his own life. Jesus' words, 'Follow me', encapsulate the call to Peter, and the vocation of every disciple, to follow him into both cross and resurrection, to hold together justice and mercy, and be agents of change in an unjust and broken world. The mystery and foolishness of the cross suggest that transformation cannot happen without pain in this world, yet that it is within the pain, anguish and struggle that the unexpected work of God blooms into more than we can imagine.

The presence of the cross in the resurrection endures beyond the resurrection appearances; the story of Thomas, asking to touch Jesus, to put his hand in his side, reminds us that the resurrected Christ still bears the scars of injustice, of his struggle against injustice and all that is wrong in a sinful world. As Jesus is taken up into

God in the Ascension, God fully absorbs the scars that go with him, and the cost of injustice and of fighting. The identification of God with his people, his commitment to relationship and bearing the pain of his people, is not temporary or ephemeral, not limited to the earthly life of Christ, but somehow, mysteriously, taken into the very heart of God.

Prayer

In holding the different themes and questions of this chapter, meditate on and pray the words of the apostle Paul in Philippians 2.1–11:

> If then there is any encouragement in Christ, any consolation from love, any sharing in the Spirit, any compassion and sympathy, make my joy complete: be of the same mind, having the same love, being in full accord and of one mind. Do nothing from selfish ambition or conceit, but in humility regard others as better than yourselves. Let each of you look not to your own interests, but to the interests of others. Let the same mind be in you that was in Christ Jesus,
>
> who, though he was in the form of God,
>   did not regard equality with God
>   as something to be exploited,
> but emptied himself,
>   taking the form of a slave,
>   being born in human likeness.
> And being found in human form,
>   he humbled himself
>   and became obedient to the point of death –
>   even death on a cross.
>
> Therefore God also highly exalted him
>   and gave him the name
>   that is above every name,
> so that at the name of Jesus

every knee should bend,
in heaven and on earth and under the earth,
and every tongue should confess
that Jesus Christ is Lord,
to the glory of God the Father.

6

'Do this to remember me'

Holy Communion and the reshaping
of the imagination

The signs of God at work, the revelation of God's nature, were there throughout Scripture for all to see. Yet, somehow, humans missed them, again and again – and still do. In Christ, God did something deeply consonant with everything already revealed, yet radically new and unexpected. This radical newness is key to reshaping the imagination when it comes to justice. The ways we think about justice are defined and limited by what we think is possible, by our culture, by the political climate around us, by upbringing and life experience. The entire system of exchanges and relationships around us teaches us that there is only so much you can do, and warns us of all the dreadful consequences of breaking out. Debates on the environment are a case in point: in a world that believes that progress is essential and inevitable, a world that teaches human beings that success equals consumption and wealth and a 'good life' has to include material blessings, a world where we are told that large multinational companies cannot be restrained easily, we hide the consequences of our actions, because it is the actions of some that lead to environmental disaster for others. It is almost impossible to imagine how to stop the self-destructive spiral of climate change. The best we can come up with is often a tweaking of the system: technological solutions and sustainable power that would enable progress to continue and lifestyles to remain undisturbed. To conceive a completely different solution is too hard, too scary, and would require such a complete change of individual lives and the workings of a globalized economy that, even if we could imagine it, making it real would be judged impossible. So we rearrange the deckchairs on the Titanic, rather than ensure that lifeboats are full and ready to go. True solutions can only be found outside of the very way of thinking that has produced oppression, destruction and acquiescence to its effects.

To imagine something new requires an intervention from the outside, a gift, and an enlargement of our imaginations so we are enabled to receive that gift. It requires us to be willing to contemplate the unimaginable, the utopian, what is foolish and beyond reason. In other words, we need God to intervene, to come into our reality and transform it with his. We need the cross and the resurrection.

The problem is, they have already happened, and human beings have not really changed. Every generation needs to meet God anew, to be confronted by the radical nature of the cross. History shows the unending ability of human beings to domesticate the cross, to pervert its message even. The New Testament Church, so close to the life of Jesus, still full of eyewitnesses, already struggled with this. The Epistle of James repeatedly impresses on the young communities that their faith has practical consequences that demand the reorganization of their lives, relationships and practices; Paul does so too, and so does John:

> But if anyone has the world's goods and sees his brother in need, yet closes his heart against him, how does God's love abide in him? Little children, let us not love in word or talk but in deed and in truth.
> (1 John 3.17–18)

Every generation has to come to know God for themselves, and experience God's leadership and transforming power. The Old Testament had much wisdom to offer. The life of Israel was to be shaped by a regular rhythm of formative worship, rituals and festivals designed to keep the memory of God alive, and shape the people to think and act in distinctive ways. The story of God's love for, and liberation of, Israel was told again and again in the

Passover, so that the people of God could be invited to lay their own story alongside the bigger story of God's revelation. The repetition of the story, the re-enactment, are all there to counteract the corrosive influence of imaginations shaped by scarcity, sin and brokenness, and foster a creative dialogue between past and present, between God's past actions and God's presence here and now.

In the same way, Jesus left his followers a shape for remembrance, a story to be repeated and re-enacted often enough that it can shape and reshape the imagination.

> For I received from the Lord what I also handed on to you, that the Lord Jesus on the night when he was betrayed took a loaf of bread, and when he had given thanks, he broke it and said, 'This is my body that is for you. Do this in remembrance of me.' In the same way he took the cup also, after supper, saying, 'This cup is the new covenant in my blood. Do this, as often as you drink it, in remembrance of me.' For as often as you eat this bread and drink the cup, you proclaim the Lord's death until he comes.
> (1 Corinthians 11.23–26)

Among many other things, Communion forms a community in the practice of justice. In both Old and New Testament, worship and justice are clearly linked. Where justice is not practised, worship is worthless, while true worship flows out into an embodiment of justice. The apostle Paul berates the Corinthian church for failing to understand that what matters is not merely that they share the Lord's Supper, but *how* they share it:

> Now in the following instructions I do not commend you, because when you come together it is not for the better but for the worse. For, to begin with, when you come together as a church, I hear that there are divisions among you; and to some extent I believe it. Indeed, there have to be factions among you, for only so will it become clear who among you are genuine. When you come together, it is not really to eat

the Lord's supper. For when the time comes to eat, each of you goes ahead with your own supper, and one goes hungry and another becomes drunk. What! Do you not have homes to eat and drink in? Or do you show contempt for the church of God and humiliate those who have nothing? What should I say to you? Should I commend you? In this matter I do not commend you!

(1 Corinthians 11.17–22)

The believers in Corinth had turned Communion into a disembodied ritual; the words had lost their meaning, because they were not embedded into the life of the community, and the community had lost sight of its vocation as a body, because it did not seek to live out the words that they prayed. How often, today, do we consider how the words and actions of Holy Communion shape and reflect the truth of our communities? How many of our churches locally have 'factions'? How many bring together some who go hungry unnoticed while others have more than they need? And if we think of the Church as a body across its local gatherings, then nationally and internationally, how do Paul's words challenge us about factions and inequality?

Discerning the body

Presiding Bishop Michael Curry, from the Episcopal Church in the USA, reflects on Paul's instructions to the Corinthians, and how they apply today:

'Do this in remembrance of me.'

These words are quite familiar to Episcopalians, and indeed to Christians of all types who have experienced a Communion service. What is probably less familiar is that the earliest mention of the Eucharist, the Lord's Supper, is found not in one of the Gospels but in the eleventh chapter of St Paul's First Letter to the Corinthians. Indeed, the apostle's recitation of Jesus' words – 'This is my body . . . This is my blood . . . Do this in remembrance of me' – predates by several years the accounts of Matthew, Mark, Luke and John.

Now Paul devoted the first ten chapters of that epistle to challenging believers in Corinth about divisions that had grown up among them, born out of an elitist sense of superiority that some seemed to wear like a badge of honour. Starting with verse 17 in chapter 11, Paul begins talking about how the opinion of some that they were somehow better or more important than others showed itself even in the context of worship, specifically the Eucharist.

Both then and now, the Lord's Supper has been intended as a service of thanksgiving to God (the Greek word *eucharistō* literally means 'to give thanks'). It also has been a special moment of fellowship for those bound together by a common faith, love and hope in Christ. Simply put, for followers of Jesus, it is the family meal. And yet, in Corinth, the wealthier, more influential church members chose not to wait for those among them who were lower on the social ladder, those who had no choice but to work longer hours, often because they were servants of the very ones who insisted on starting the common meal without them. This meal of solidarity, a feast ironically called *agapē*, meaning 'love,' had become instead another occasion of neglect, just looking out for number one.

Paul was incensed . . . and for good reason. How could those who claimed to be part of the Jesus Movement ever transform an unjust, uncompassionate world when they themselves were not displaying justice and compassion among themselves! Make no mistake: this was not about theological differences or political divisions. The problem here was a choice by some to put their own needs before the well-being of their siblings in Christ. This was not a question of whether some believed the world revolved around the sun, but the fact that some acted as if the world revolved around them.

'Do this in remembrance of me.' The opposite of love is not hate . . . but selfishness. The problem in Corinth then, and the problems in our world now, are because we fail to remember what is truly important for any who would dare to follow the Jesus of the Gospels, the Jesus who preached the Sermon on the Mount, the Jesus who reached out to outsiders, the Jesus who forgave his enemies, the Jesus who laid down his life for the sake of others. The problem, then and now, is that we forget love. And where love is absent, so too is justice.

Paul quotes Jesus' words of institution – 'This is my body . . . This is my blood . . . Do this in remembrance of me' – but then follows up with a challenge. 'Examine yourselves, and only then eat of the bread and drink of the cup. For all who eat and drink without discerning the body, eat and drink judgement against themselves' (1 Corinthians 11.28–29). In case we are tempted to think of the 'body' he is referring to only in terms of the sacramental bread, note that Paul goes on in chapter 12 to talk at length about how the followers of Jesus are an interconnected body and that those who feel themselves to be superior in some way should give 'the greater honour to the inferior member,' so that 'the members may have the same care for one another' (12.24b–25). Or as the American Prayer Book puts it, 'We remember before you all poor and neglected persons whom it would be easy for us to forget' (TEC, 2006).

By moving from a rebuke of the selfishness exhibited
by some members of the body during the eucharistic feast
to the exquisite yet wholly practical description of love in
1 Corinthians 13, the Holy Spirit through Paul calls all of
us who follow Jesus to dare to do just that . . . to follow his
example in all that we do. Nineteen centuries later, the Revd
Dr Martin Luther King Jr, in one of his letters, wrote, 'Love is
the heartbeat of the moral cosmos.' Anyone who loves, Dr King
says, 'is a participant in the being of God'.

So let us indeed, as participants in the being of God, do all
this in remembrance of Jesus.

Let us do justice in remembrance of Jesus.

Let us do compassion in remembrance of Jesus.

Let us do love in remembrance of Jesus.

And let the world be transformed through us.

Holy Communion has always been a contested site, precisely
because it demands so much of us. It demands that we attend to
the unity that is given to us by Jesus: we are his people, his Church,
his body. The Church is not formed by human choice but by God's
gift; as such, every Christian is a gift of God to the other. Hence the
barriers erected by class, culture and all the differences that human
beings use to categorize, make hierarchies, assign worth, and justify
inequalities and the distances they create, are just this: barriers. In
coming together to share a meal around the risen Christ, we are
gathered as the disciples were around Jesus. They too were a motley
bunch, people who did not quite fit together, yet gathered by Christ.
Sitting down together at the table proclaims a reality much deeper
than our differences would suggest. But the discrepancy between
these two realities – our unity in Christ and our lived experience
of conflict, inequality and divisions – chafes and challenges, and
forces us either to divorce Communion from its deeper meaning,
over-spiritualize it, turn it into a privatized celebration of individual
faith; or, in more constructive settings, to examine our lives and
relationships with those who are visible, and those who are not, and
work towards closing the gap between our two realities.

In many places and times, the gap yawns wide. Small communion cups, rather than the common cup, were used in various churches to keep different groups apart: black Christians from white Christians in segregated churches in the United States, or Christians of different castes in India. The demand to be part of the body of Christ on an equal footing, equally loved, equally human, and joined together, was too challenging. Communion came to reflect and solidify injustice and division, rather than confront them. These are sharp examples, but there are subtle forms of the same behaviour: churches that mostly attract certain socio-economic groups, for instance, so that inequality is not visible when the people gather, yet still divides the body of Christ. Ultimately, the words of Paul sharply come to mind, that we should 'discern the body': who is present as we share in the Lord's Supper? Who is absent? Who might we not even realize is absent, because they are invisible to our community? Who is excluded, knowingly or unwittingly?

The reality of a broken body, before we even come to share in the broken body of Christ, may be (and should be) distressing and uncomfortable. Yet at the same time, the very brokenness of the Church as it comes to Communion proclaims that brokenness is not the end of the road; Christ is present despite our frailties and his presence embodies hope within brokenness. The Church is gathered around Christ not because it is worthy, but because it is not, and knows its need for redemption.

Questions for reflection

1 How well does your church reflect your wider community? How does it relate to other churches in the area?
2 Are there any factions, cliques or divisions within your local church? How and why did they arise?
3 Who might be absent from Communion in your local church? Who may feel excluded? Who might be invisible?

The practice of truth-telling

Communion services, in most Christian churches, will share some distinctive common features. One of these is a time of confession, through shared words or silent prayer. Confession proclaims that the Church knows it is in need of redemption, that its members and their life together are far from perfect. Confession is an invitation to approach the table in truth. If sin, as reflected in the creation narratives, is partly about human beings grasping for a radically false place within the world, then confession is about recognizing who they truly are. This reality is set within the framework of their worth and dignity, and being loved by God. But love cannot be divorced from justice, or from the claims of others upon us. Recognizing truth is the first step on the road to transformation.

Confession can be domesticated: privatized, reduced to these things we can manage, or consider changing. How can we enable uncomfortable truths to emerge in our times of confession and confront us, individually and communally? I have often heard leaders invite the congregation to have a moment of silence to think back about the previous day or week, and bring to God things done or left undone, that we carry guilt and shame about. There is certainly an important place for self-examination in truth-telling. But when it comes to justice, it may let us off the hook a bit too easily. What is the significance of coming *together* and acknowledging our failings before God? There is a place in confession not just to consider individual lives, but the failings and distortions of our life together. What is the truth of life together for this church, in this place? How are relationships distorted and damaged, maybe at times damaging?

Going beyond the church community, in confession there is a chance to acknowledge sin as far, far more than things we consciously choose to do that we have the power not to do. As we confess together, we can make space to acknowledge how we have been shaped by things done to us, by culture, upbringing, choices, that distort our lives together and further afield. We can make space to acknowledge the social, political and economic structures and systems we are part of, that we may have no power to change, yet contribute to and at times benefit from: climate change, economic inequality, global trade systems . . . As we come together and tell the truth about our lives, and ask for God to come and change them, we can also name the differential impact of all these systems on members of the body of Christ: the different impact of racist, sexist or ablist cultures and systems, of homophobic behaviour, of class-based prejudice. Christians do not exist in a vacuum, but are part of wider systems and societies whose faults and impact they are called to bring to God in truth, repentance and lament.

Truth-telling is an essential component of justice; injustice masks its own impact, and silences its victims. Confession ahead of Communion is a reminder that we are embodied people, with a vocation within the wider world. Our worship is not confined to the building it happens in, but concerns the whole of our lives, gathered and dispersed. In confession, we call for justice, and recognize our part in its absence, in the knowledge that the God of all truth is ready to meet our pain and brokenness with his embrace. As we do so, we come as equals before God – in our need of grace, our longing for justice, and our belovedness.

Confession, fortunately, is not the end of the road, but the beginning. Once we tell the truth of our world, and our participation in its brokenness, it is natural to move into a prayer for change, a prayer of solidarity with those whose distress has been named and witnessed to. This is the other side of truth-telling: the recognition that what is is not what should be, and that remedy is possible, because God is at work within us, and within the world. The turn to prayer further acknowledges that the search for justice, for remedy, is not one we can undertake alone, but must be pursued with God and shaped by his purposes.

Justice: A Christian Palestinian perspective

A perspective on confession, forgiveness and justice from the Middle East, by the Most Revd Dr Hosam E. Naoum, Anglican Archbishop in Jerusalem.

As we have seen throughout the earlier chapters of this volume, the concept of justice is unquestionably a fundamental part of our Christian faith. This is certainly evident throughout the Old Testament, from Deuteronomy's pronouncement of 'Justice, and only justice, you shall pursue' (Deuteronomy 16.20) to Micah's pronouncement, 'What does the LORD require of you but to do justice, and to walk humbly with your God?' (Micah 6.8). In this last passage, however, earlier chapters have also observed that the prophet balances the notion of justice with that of mercy, where one walks before God in all humility.

Yet if mercy is to be granted, justice must still be served, as sin carries a heavy price. Prophetic reflection upon this theological dilemma eventually led to the vision of a messianic figure – the Suffering Servant – who endured injustice on behalf of those whom God would show mercy (Isaiah 52.13—53.12).

For Christians, these verses serve as part of the prophetic foundation for our understanding of Jesus' messianic identity and redemptive mission. Christ is seen as the Paschal sacrifice on behalf of humanity's sins (1 Corinthians 5.7–8), a sacrifice willingly and lovingly made by him on the cross (Ephesians 4.2). Christ's resurrection was a vindication of his righteousness (Acts 2.14–36), with his single sacrifice for sins being followed by his elevation to the right hand of God and the sanctification of those who come before his throne in faith (Hebrews 10.12ff.). The ones who stand before him in repentance receive forgiveness of their sins (Romans 3.4; Colossians 1.13–14).

Coupled with this message of divine forgiveness is also a call to forgive as one has been forgiven (e.g. Mark 11.25; Matthew 6.14–15). The centrality of this teaching is seen in its prominent place within the Lord's Prayer, which contains the petition 'and forgive us our debts, as we also have forgiven our debtors' (Matthew 6.12).

Yet because the offering of forgiveness is one of the most difficult callings that Christians face, it is one that requires constant repentance on the part of the individual believer, whereby we seek God's forgiveness of our own sins, as well as the grace to impart that same forgiveness to those who have offended against us.

Here in the Middle East, the prevalence of the Eastern Orthodox traditions has led to the widespread devotional use of sacred icons by many Christians, including those of us in the Anglican Church. One of the most famous of all ancient icons is located in St Catherine's Monastery in the middle of the Sinai Desert. It is a sixth-century depiction of *Christos Pantocrator*, painted by an unknown master iconographer using the encaustic technique.

When first gazing upon this icon, one immediately notices something quite striking about it: the two sides of Christ's face display completely different expressions. The left side is stern and reproachful. Christ's eye stares at you in judgement. In contrast, the right side displays an expression of compassion, with Christ's right eye exuding mercy and forgiveness.

Fr Justin, the Librarian of St Catherine's Monastery, once explained that when the venerator approaches this icon, he or she should first gaze at the left side of Christ's face. This half represents God's righteous judgement and should call to mind our sins – the ways we have failed to live into Christ's teaching, as represented by the Book of Gospels held in Christ's left hand.

This look of reproach should eventually lead the worshipper to repentance and the confession of sins. At the point of contrition, the venerator should then gaze at Christ's right eye, the eye of mercy and compassion, noticing also the Saviour's right hand raised in a sign of blessing. This reveals the grace of God's forgiveness to the penitent. Upon receiving this forgiveness, the venerator should then be reminded of Christ's call to forgive as we have been forgiven. He or she should in turn go and seek to be reconciled with any estranged brother or sister.

While it is difficult to speak of a single Palestinian Christian perspective on the concept of justice, for me, this is where it all begins: in the recognizing of one's own sins, which in turn leads to repentance, followed by a receiving of God's merciful forgiveness and a movement towards seeking reconciliation with one's disaffected neighbour.

Nowhere in Palestine, perhaps, is this perspective more on display than at the Tent of Nations, a 100-acre farm south-west of Bethlehem, owned since 1916 by the Nassar family, who are of the Lutheran tradition. Over several decades, this farm has been increasingly surrounded by the Gush Etzion block of Israeli settlements, ones that are constructed on occupied territory in violation of international law.

Because the nearby settlers would like to absorb the Nassar property into their settlement block, they have relentlessly pursued all means of forcing the family off their ancestral land. These have included not only the filing of petitions to have their private land declared as public property, but also the blocking of egress to their property, the bulldozing of 1,500 of their fruit trees, and the regular torching of hundreds more.

Despite facing this extreme persecution, the Nassar family refuses to return hate with hate. As the welcome sign on their property proclaims: 'We Refuse to Be Enemies.' While defending in court their just right to their property, the family simultaneously sees their primary Christian mission as one of reconciliation. This is seen in their Statement of Goals:

> At Tent of Nations, we seek to embody a positive approach to conflict and occupation. Faced with great injustice, we know that we should not hate, despair, or flee. We can refuse to be enemies and channel our pain and frustration into positive actions which will build a better future. We aim to help the oppressed and margin-alized realize that they are powerful. We all have a role in creating the future we want to see. At Tent of Nations, we seek to work with others in the local area to lay the foun-dations for a future Palestine, in the belief that justice and peace will grow from the bottom up. We work to

reconnect people with the land. Through mixing our hands with the soil, we learn to value and understand the significance of our environment.[4]

To this end, the family not only farms their property, but they also run numerous work camps devoted to the care of creation and the fostering of peacebuilding. These are open to both local and international groups, offering a uniquely Palestinian Christian perspective of how justice and mercy operate on the ground.

This perspective reminds us that Christians cannot exercise their faith in isolation. Justice and mercy must be worked out not merely as some sort of intellectual exercise, but as part of one's active ministry within the world. Here we must remember that the Lord's Prayer is written not in the first person *singular*, but in the first person *plural*:

Our Father, who art in heaven, hallowed be thy name . . . give us this day *our* daily bread, and forgive *us our* trespasses as *we* forgive those who trespass against *us* . . . and lead *us* not into temptation, but deliver *us* from evil . . .

Even if we do not always recognize it, in this prayer we are praying not merely for ourselves, but on behalf of our neighbours as well.

And so, from this Palestinian Christian perspective, justice does not stand alone. As the prophet Micah so aptly put it in an oracle that our Lord Jesus Christ himself personified, God's justice cannot be separated from his mercy, for in Christ we find both perfectly manifested. Moreover, justice and mercy, while emanating from the Almighty, are intended to be bestowed upon humanity as a collective entity – one throughout which God seeks complete reconciliation, for we are all indeed his beloved children, bound together as members of the larger human family.

---

4 'About Us', Tent of Nations, <www.tentofnations.org/about/about-us/>, accessed 23 June 2021.

Take, eat, this is my body

Maybe the most obvious thing about Communion, though often something we hardly think about, is quite how *physical* it is. The story of Jesus is recounted in some way, but the very centre of Communion is not words or concepts. It is the gathering of the people together, the breaking and sharing of bread and wine, eating and drinking. Community is an embodied practice. Bread and wine are linked to hunger and thirst, the two most basic indicators of poverty; their absence is almost always unequal, and hoarding them forms the beginning of injustice. Food and drink are the condition of life. Bread is a staple, and in places without safe sources of water, wine is a safe form of hydration. It is easy in comfortable surroundings to forget the meaning of either, or reduce them to a purely spiritual meaning. The power of the symbols of bread and wine, however, lies precisely in the way they bridge the spiritual and the physical. They proclaim that worship has got to be embedded into the whole of life. The fact that they are shared together, that Communion cannot be taken on one's own, is an inescapable call to justice; it is not about feeding the self, but about sharing equally within the body. In Communion, I am not just linked to other Christians on a spiritual level, but I am physically and practically bound to them. A thick network of mutual love and responsibility is formed, and a question lingers: does the sharing we practise in Communion reflect the truth of our relationships, or is our sharing and bonding limited to this point of contact between us?

We cannot say that justice matters unless we think that bodies matter: their health, their vulnerability, their differences and the way these differences prompt discrimination. In order to address injustice, we need to see the bodies of those who suffer, and value them. Communion calls us to see bodies, to acknowledge their call upon us and their relevance to our faith. And if we see them truthfully, then we are called to act for their good. The words of Jesus repeated in Communion services go one step further: 'Take, eat, this is my body, broken for you.' In these simple words we find again the embrace of God towards humanity. The choice to enter human flesh, to identify with his broken creatures, and in turn become broken for them.

The simplicity of bread and wine are further encouragements to the practice of justice. Bread reminds us of the miracles of Jesus, and the abundance in the feeding of the five thousand. That story, in Mark, was contrasted to an elaborate banquet. The crowd is fed in simplicity, and everyone eats their fill, while leftovers are taken away. There is no hoarding, and no difference in provision. Together with God's abundance comes a certain restraint, an invitation to take what is needed and no more. The simplicity of bread and wine is an antidote to an imagination that justifies giving much to some and little to others, banquets for some, hunger for others. The simplicity speaks against hoarding, against luxury and the exploitation of creation for ever more resources. As the people come to the table, they all receive equally, of the same bread and wine, of the basic fare needed to sustain life. Communion suggests appropriate boundaries for human desires, so that all can share equally. Once again, the very act of sharing together both shapes our imagination of what should be – a radical equality and a minimum standard of access to the basics of life – and exposes our faults: how is the equality we proclaim in ritual matched in our lives together? How is the equality in our lives together matched in our belonging in the wider world?

The practice of Communion proclaims a vision that answers the truth-telling of confession and the requests of intercession. The gestures of Communion, the food we share, the gathering of a community of equals, enact and proclaim the relationships of a different economy. The answer is embodied, interpersonal, it is about the meeting of persons and their acceptance of what their mutual relationships could and should be. As Scripture is read or quoted in liturgy, the story of God and his people is told in many ways, and anchors the community into a living tradition, the continual action of God throughout history. This tradition, this story, is then appropriated by the community of faith today – and therein lies Communion's greatest challenge to us. How do we let this story transform today's stories? How does the story we tell in

Communion – of what Jesus did, and what he does, now, in the service – speak into the truth-telling of confession? How does it help us move from intercession to action?

Questions for reflection

1 Archbishop Michael Ramsey once wrote: 'The supreme question is not what we make of the Eucharist, but what the Eucharist is making of us, as together with the Word of God it fashions us into the way of Christ.'
2 What do you think the Eucharist makes of you, as an individual? Of your local church? Your national church? The Church everywhere, today?
3 How might ongoing reflection on the Eucharist shape your own life, and the life of your local church?

Allowing the truth-telling of confession to be brought into Communion helps sharpen some of its challenges and questions – and maybe reveal new truths; the world of confession and intercessions cannot be left at the door, or forgotten during Communion. Instead, Communion shapes and reshapes us so that we respond in ways rooted in the story and ways of God. Communion both challenges and readies us to turn to the world that Jesus loved and came to save. Communion, however, also proclaims that the body of Christ was broken, and it is only through that brokenness that we can be gathered in truth and justice. The practice of Communion is a clear safeguard against the temptation of triumphalism, or the kind of heroism that seeks to overcome injustice through sheer power. Communion shapes us for justice because it reminds us, again and again, that the way of justice goes through the cross. And as we are sent out, at the end of a service, to love and serve the Lord, it is a call to go, not in our own strength, not to lead the world to a better place, but a call to follow Christ, and his example of costly compassion.

Communion reminds us of the whole story of God and the people of earth, encapsulated in the story of Jesus. It is a story that starts with people created equal, with dignity, dearly loved, and a story that calls us, incessantly, to live out that love in faithfulness to the image of God within us. It is this love, the start and end of all things, that makes the call, the difficulties of transform-ation and the way of the cross, bearable. It is love alone that can hold justice and mercy in one, transformative embrace, which whispers to the world, you are loved, and you are not alone. It is this immense love of God that gives us motivation and purpose to explore our vocation to reflect him more fully, keeps us going when we get it wrong, and assures us that God is already at work for justice and mercy, long before we even realize that either are needed. It is God's embrace of our humanity, in love and grace, that prepares and charges us to embrace justice for ourselves, for our broken world, and embrace our neighbour, so we can love them as ourselves.

Prayer

Our Father in heaven,
who embraces your broken, sinful and suffering people

Hallowed be your name,
a name that speaks of justice, peace and compassion

Your kingdom come,
a kingdom of justice and peace; may it bring down oppressive empires of our making

Your will be done,
and may we recognize when we confuse our will with yours

On earth as in heaven,
and may we discern and nurture the seeds of your kingdom already among us

Give us today our daily bread,
help us take only what is ours, so that we do not hoard for tomorrow the bread that our neighbour needs today

open the eyes of those who have much, that all may have bread and none go hungry

Forgive us our sins
our greed, our unwillingness to see and love our neighbour, all the things we do not even see or know about ourselves, our communities and our world

As we forgive those who sin against us
help us work towards justice and not revenge, and show us how grace can transform both ourselves, and the ones we cannot bear to love

Lead us not into temptation
the temptation to exploit or condemn, the temptation to dehumanise those we despise or disagree with, the temptation to ask more of the other than we ask of ourselves

But deliver us from evil,
deliver us from the evil we visit on others, and the evil visited upon us; deliver us from the evils of slavery, of exploitation, of dehumanisation, of discrimination in all its forms

For the kingdom, the power and the glory are yours, forever and ever.
Amen.

What now?

The task of justice is never-ending, and the practice of Holy Communion, together with reading the Scriptures, reminds us constantly that it is our vocation, as the people of God, to keep pursuing justice. How we do this will be as varied as there are people, and churches and contexts. If there is one thing we learn from the Bible's stories of justice, it is that justice is multi-faceted, complex and, all too often, elusive. It is a vocation, something we constantly have to grow into and discover. Justice is not just liberation, or equality, or laws, or personal relationship. It is all these things, together, and more. In order to discover how to do justly today in our communities, we need to listen to what God is saying, in humility, and meet the people whose lives we must embrace: people like us, in many ways. They may look different from us, have different lives, loves and priorities, and we may, in our heads, put them in different boxes that say 'victims' or 'oppressed', or 'oppressor'; they may be good or bad or in-between, or, more likely, a mix of all three. But fundamentally, at the root of all things, they are people made in the image of God, like you and me, who need God's loving and challenging embrace. It is only when meeting them truly, openly, in the presence of God, that we can start to move towards justice.

The human propensity to do injustice, together with the fluidity of human cultures and contexts, also means that we can never sit back and say, 'It is done.' New ways of doing justice, new people to meet and embrace, are always calling. With every step, we discover that the 'justice' of yesterday created some of the unforeseen 'injustices' of today. It is easy to be discouraged by the task, but we keep before us the One whose words on the cross were, 'It is finished.' We may be growing towards justice, but on the cross Jesus has accomplished what we cannot. The fight for justice is not an open contest between cosmic powers of equal might. It is a fight God has already won, and is inviting us to join, on his terms: by letting ourselves be embraced by his love, and choosing, in turn, to love our neighbour and embrace them, with justice and mercy, with truth and gentleness, with firmness and humility, for, in the embrace, we discover that we are not so different after all. We are all made in the image of God, and called to live in ways that allow this image to shine and transform the world around.

Then, truly, we may say

'let justice roll down like waters,
    and righteousness like an ever-flowing stream.'
(Amos 5.24)

Bibliography

Bills, N., 2020, *A Theology of Justice in Exodus, Siphrut 26*, University Park, PA: Eisenbrauns.

Bonhoeffer, D., 2015 (1st edn 1949), *The Cost of Discipleship*, London: SCM Press.

Brueggemann, W., 1982, *The Creative Word*, Philadelphia, PA: Fortress.

Brueggemann, W., 2018, *The Prophetic Imagination, 40th Anniversary Edition*, Minneapolis, MN: Fortress.

Douglass, Frederick, 2009 (1st edn 1845), *Narrative of the Life of Frederick Douglass by Frederick Douglass, an American Slave* (Oxford World Classics), Oxford: Oxford University Press.

Evans, Paul S., 2015, 'Imagining Justice for the Marginalized: A suspicious reading of the Covenant Code (Exodus 21:1—23:33) in its Ancient Near Eastern Context', in Westfall, C. L. and Dyer, B. R. (eds), *The Bible and Social Justice: Old Testament and New Testament foundations for the Church's urgent call*, Eugene, OR: Wipf and Stock, pp. 1–34.

Forrester, Duncan, 2001, *On Human Worth: A Christian vindication of equality*, London: SCM Press.

Lynch, M., 2020, *Portraying Violence in the Hebrew Bible*, Cambridge: Cambridge University Press.

Obama, Barack, 1995, *Dreams from My Father*, New York: Times Books.

Sacks, J., 1995, *Faith in the Future*, London: Darton, Longman and Todd.

Sacks, J., 2002, *The Dignity of Difference*, London: Continuum.

Sacks, J., 2010, *Covenant and Conversation: A weekly reading of the Jewish Bible; Exodus: The book of redemption*, New Milford, CT: Maggid Books.

The Episcopal Church (TEC), 2006, The Book of Common Prayer: Together with the Psalter, or Psalms of David, Ann Arbor, MI: Scholarly Publishing Office, University of Michigan Library.

Volf, M., 1996, *Exclusion and Embrace: A theological exploration of identity, otherness and reconciliation*, Nashville, TN: Abingdon.

WE HAVE A VISION OF A WORLD IN WHICH EVERYONE IS TRANSFORMED BY CHRISTIAN KNOWLEDGE

As well as being an award-winning publisher, SPCK is the oldest Anglican mission agency in the world.

Our mission is to lead the way in creating books and resources that help everyone to make sense of faith.

Will you partner with us to put good books into the hands of prisoners, great assemblies in front of schoolchildren and reach out to people who have not yet been transformed by the Christian faith?

To donate, please visit www.spckpublishing.co.uk/donate or call our friendly fundraising team on 020 7592 3900.

The Big Church Read

Did you know that you can read

Embracing Justice

as a Big Church Read?

Join together with friends, your small group or your whole church, or do it on your own, as Isabelle Hamley leads you through the book.

Visit www.thebigchurchread.co.uk or use the QR code below to watch exclusive videos from Isabelle Hamley as she explores the ideas and themes of *Embracing Justice*.

The Big Church Read will also provide you with a reading plan and discussion questions to help guide you through the book.

It's free to join in and a great way to read through *Embracing Justice*!